ELITE PERFORMANCE

Cycling

SUCCESSFUL SPORTIVES

ELITE PERFORMANCE

Cycling

SUCCESSFUL SPORTIVES

Dr Garry Palmer & Richard Allen

A & C BLACK • LONDON

For the Bs in my life. Love you.

First published in 2008 by
A&C Black Publishers Ltd
38 Soho Square, London W1D 3HB
www.acblack.com

ISBN 9781408100493

A CIP catalogue record for this book is available from the British Library.

Typeset in MetaPlusNormal by Palimpsest Book Production Limited, Grangemouth, Stirlingshire

Inside photography © Richard Allen p3, 30, 33, 56 (top and bottom left), 100; © Gerard Brown 6, 40, 118, 158, 169; © Jeff Edwards 20, 65, 67, 68; © Tina Howe 126; © Brian Jones, Kimroy Photography 89; © kenesisbikes.co.uk 44; © Andrew Kennedy/ kennedyimages.co.uk ii; © Maindru Photo, France 23; © Garry Palmer 14, 35, 72, 73, 77, 78, 149, 162; © scienceinsport.com 136; © scott-sports.com 45; © Bryan Taylor 109-116; © Andy Whitehouse 1, 2, 38, 56 (bottom right)
Cover photography © istockphoto

Printed and bound by South China Printing Co.

This book is produced using paper that is made from wood grown in managed, sustainable forests. It is natural, renewable and recyclable. The logging and manufacturing processes conform to the environmental regulations of the country of origin.

CONTENTS

PART THREE: NUTRITION

PART FOUR: THE BIG DAY

ACKNOWLEDGEMENTS

Hugh Porter MBE has been of great assistance and the authors are grateful for his input and for the fact that one of the leading figures in the sport was willing to write a foreword for this book. We would also like to thank Mark Cavendish, who also wrote a foreword, and provided some great insights into the world of professional cycle racing. Mark, along with Malcolm Elliott, Jonny Bellis and Peter Kennaugh Jnr have all given their time and advice generously, and have provided valuable comments for various sections in the book.

A special mention must also go to all the non-elite riders who have freely contributed their time and experience of sportive events worldwide. Without you, this book would not have had such a colourful wealth of information about the rides available. Some of you have been featured in sections of the book, others were just happy to help and contribute. You are far too numerous to mention by name, so thank you to you all, you know who you are.

Thanks also to freelance photographers Andy Whitehouse (AMW Photography) and Brian Jones (Kimroy Photography) and Bryan Taylor for their kind permission to use some of their pictures. We would also like to express our gratitude to those who provided data to be used in the book. Specifically SRM for the power information from elite riders in the Tour de France; Scott bikes and Kenesis bikes for information about their products; Science in Sport for unpublished nutritional information; and to the various academic journals who have kindly agreed to allow us to reproduce previously published information.

Richard would like to thank everyone involved in the Isle of Man cycling community for their assistance. Also helpful were Isle of Man national coach Mike Doyle and Ellan Vannin, CC's Steve Shimmin. The following are also Manx cycling enthusiasts, coaches and journalists who have been of great assistance: John Watterson and Mike Wade (Isle of Man Newspapers); Peter Kennaugh Snr (Manx Road Club); Jonny Bellis Snr; Gary Hines (IoM National Team Manager); Ben and Isla Scott; Ollie Last, Ian Brand, Chris Whorrall; and Mark Christian and everyone at the Bikestyle shop in Douglas.

Thanks also to James Pope and Camilla Seers at Face Partnership; everyone at Fred Williams Cycles in Wolverhampton; Andy Cook and Phil Ingham at British Cycling and to Graham Baxter Sporting Tours. A massive thank you must also go to Jo McRae for all her hard work in preparing the section on stretching and flexibility. Your input was invaluable.

Finally, thank you to all at A&C Black for making this book possible: the many who have offered advice, helped with the proof reading, and clarity of content, and to those that have put up with our high levels of stress throughout the whole process.

Never again . . . well maybe.

FOREWORD

By pro rider Mark Cavendish

Mark Cavendish during the Tour de France in 2007

Mark Cavendish won 11 races in his first season as a pro rider with the T-Mobile team in 2007, including stage wins in the Tour of Catalonia and Tour of Britain. On the track he won the Madison title with Rob Hayles at the 2005 World Championships and became Commonwealth Games scratch race champion in 2006.

Cycling is one of the toughest sports there is. And endurance events on the road are demanding for professional cyclists and club riders alike. Whether your goal is to win a professional race or achieve a goal you have set yourself in a sportive event, it will require dedication and determination if you are to produce the best performance possible.

Training in all weathers and pushing yourself to stick to a training plan even when you feel like giving up are experiences we all share, whatever level we compete at. Even elite riders sometimes feel like quitting when they're struggling to find form or have bad luck in a race. But what keeps us all going when we are soaked through and freezing cold on a winter training ride is the thought of what we are training for. And when we achieve the goal we have set ourselves, all that training and self-sacrifice is worthwhile.

For me cycling is something I love doing. Being paid to do something I love is a bonus. But if I wasn't a professional I would still be out there on my bike and racing. So I can understand the growing appeal of cyclosportive events like the Étape du Tour, which allow club riders the chance to experience for themselves a little of what it is like to ride races like the Tour de France.

I made my debut in the Tour de France in 2007, hoping to pick up some wins in sprint finishes. But I also had my first taste of Tour mountain stages in the Alps. Although I had ridden many big races as an amateur and as a pro, I entered another world in the Tour. In the Alps I had to push myself harder than ever before to get over the big cols. It was a great experience and in years to come I hope to make more progress in the world's greatest bike race.

And I hope that what you'll learn from this book about advances in sports science and training will help you achieve your goal.

FOREWORD

By ex-pro rider and four-time world professional pursuit champion Hugh Porter

Hugh Porter

Hugh Porter MBE was four times the world professional pursuit champion and also a successful road racer, competing against the legendary Eddy Merckx. For more than 20 years, Hugh has been the BBC's voice of cycling, commentating on all the major events.

Ever since I began riding a bike as an 11-year-old, my life has revolved around cycling. As a competitor, the sport took me around the globe to World Championships, the Olympics and the Commonwealth Games. When I retired from racing I entered the world of broadcasting, which allowed me to continue my involvement.

At the age of 67 I still have the passion and love for cycling that inspired me to take up the sport all those years ago. It has brought me a lifetime of enjoyment, and a lot of friends who share my enthusiasm. I even met my wife through cycling!

Such is the camaraderie among cyclists that, wherever you go in the world, if you are on a bike you will have friends the moment you meet someone else on two wheels. So the tremendous success of British cycling in recent years, and the boom in sportive rides like the Étape du Tour, is something which I warmly welcome.

The great thing about sportive rides is that they have encouraged so many more people to discover cycling as a way of keeping fit or as a way of entering the world of road racing. Some of you may be taking up sportive riding to raise money for charity or simply because you like a challenge. Maybe you have watched the Tour de France on TV, or have seen the greatest race of them all while on holiday and want to find out what it is like to ride a mountain stage.

Whatever your reason for wanting to ride a sportive event, I am sure this book will be useful in helping you to achieve your goal. Cycling is a simple pleasure, but recent advances in training methods mean that, to make the most of the time you have available for training, you need to really analyse your preparation. Ultimately it is up to you to get out and train for your chosen event. But with the expert advice in these pages you can ensure that you arrive on the start line knowing that you have done everything possible to prepare yourself for the challenge ahead.

I wish you every success, and hope that you gain as much enjoyment from the sport as it has given me over the last half-century.

PREFACE: LIVING THE DREAM
RICHARD ALLEN

'We know why men go off to war. But it is harder to explain why a few might want to attempt a profession in which the suffering is so internalised. Are they masochists? If not, why the hell are they doing it? In the mountains the question becomes suddenly luminous. One has only to look around at the awesome surroundings; at the millions gathered so far from where they live; and at these little figures approaching up the vertiginous bends of a pass. There is something called glory and here on these heights these riders are in the process of attaining it.'

Richard Allen

Author Robin Magowan captures the magic of mountain stages of the Tour de France in his book *Kings of the Road*.

The Étape du Tour: it's like riding the Tour de France in one day. It was the appeal of the Tour that inspired the Étape du Tour event, which has led to a boom in sportive riding across the world.

All the hopes and dreams, triumph and despair, fear and elation experienced by the world's top riders in the world's greatest bike race are shared by competitors in the Étape. Like many of you, my motivation for riding the Étape was to get a taste of what it must be like to ride in the Tour de France. I wanted to live the dream, to ride a stage on closed roads and with villages along the route packed with fans cheering you on just as they would when the Tour de France

passed by a few days later. Only an elite few can ride the Tour for real; for the rest of us, the Étape is as close as we are ever going to get to sharing in the glory of the race.

My own fascination with the Tour de France began in the 1980s when I watched Robert Millar and Stephen Roche leading the wave of English-speaking riders who changed the face of continental racing. And it was during the mountain stages, seeing riders push themselves to the limit up the classic climbs in the Alps and Pyrenees or on the vicious ascent of Mont Ventoux, that I became captivated by the Tour.

It is arguably the toughest endurance event in the world and it's in the mountains that you see

3

the elite athletes in the Tour define the meaning of determination. Mountain stages can be up to 140 km (87 miles) long and include four or five cols. In between the climbs, there are descents where riders will top 96 km/h (60 mph). To make it more difficult, the high mountains can be tackled in freezing rain or 37.7˚C (100˚F) heat.

Just to get to the finish of stages like this requires not just physical fitness but mental strength too. It is a test of character, a test of self-discipline in training and of courage in competition. It requires the athlete to reach down into their very soul to dredge up every last ounce of energy. In the mountains there are no hiding places, and no room for excuses. The mountains will judge you, and their verdict is measured in unforgiving hours and minutes.

By the time you cross the finish line, your soul has been stripped bare after reaching the point of physical and mental exhaustion. Anyone who tackles stages like this, whether they are Tour champions or club riders, finds out something about who they are. You also find out how your performance measures against the legends of the sport. For me, this was the main reason for wanting to take up the challenge of the Étape du Tour and it was a motivation for this book.

Sportive rides are hard and it's not easy for cyclists with busy lives to be able to fit in the training they require to reach their goals. So our aim in this book is to ensure that you make the most of the time you have available and get the best out of yourself in whatever event you choose to ride, be it a sportive, a charity cycling event or a competitive race.

Read, learn and live your dream!

1

THE LURE OF CYCLOSPORTIVE

1

REALISING YOUR POTENTIAL

Be the best that you can be

For many years cyclists would sit watching the Tour de France on TV and wonder what it would be like to ride a Tour stage in the Alps or Pyrenees. In 1993 the Étape du Tour was launched and everyone got that chance. Following the route of a mountainous stage of the Tour de France, just a few days before the professional riders covered the same route, the Étape du Tour not only gave amateur riders and enthusiasts a taste of the life of a pro, it set the standard for sportive rides and has inspired similar events around the world. The last few years have seen an explosion in sportive events, with tens of thousands of cyclists taking up the challenge.

Sportive rides offer something for everyone, from those aiming to win to others just wanting to complete the route within the time limit. Many sportives have the added appeal of being raced over routes of big professional races like the Tour de France or Giro d'Italia. Races like the Étape are respected events in their own right with some winners even going on to compete in the Tour de France proper.

French rider Christophe Rinero won the first Étape du Tour before turning pro. In 1998, riding for the Cofidis team, he finished fourth in the Tour de France and won the King of the Mountains prize. When their pro careers are over, many riders can't resist reliving some of their former glory by turning out in the Étape. Five-time Tour de France winner Miguel Indurain, and three-time Tour champion Greg Lemond, have both ridden in the Étape in recent years.

For me (Garry) the Étape experience is something I will never forget. My first event was in 2002 in the French Alps and I will always remember the first big climb I faced – the Cormet de Roseland. It was 19 km (12 miles) to the top; that's about 16 km (10 miles) longer than anything I had previously climbed. Feeling my ears pop halfway up suddenly made me realise that these climbs were a lot tougher than Tour de France riders made them look when I watched them on TV.

But swooping down the other side of the mountain at 80 km/h (50 mph), through ski villages full of cheering spectators clanging Alpine cow bells, made it all worthwhile. Being swept along in a multinational peloton, with everyone riding in a common cause even though most of us couldn't speak a word of each other's language, is something else that is special about the Étape.

Big sportives offer a chance to race in a peloton of thousands, far more appealing to many riders than a local Sunday morning race of a few dozen. Riders dropped by the leaders after a few kilometres in your local Sunday morning club race face a long, lonely ride to the finish. In most sportive events there will always be someone to ride with. Often you will find yourself in a peloton bigger than that in the Tour de France itself!

Sportive riding has caused a massive boom in cycling. For most participants, the challenge of a cyclosportive is to get to the finish or to improve their finishing position from previous years. Sportives are challenging, but you don't

necessarily have to train 20 hours a week to be able to achieve your goal.

But how do you make the most of the time you do have to train? There are many books on the market offering advice about training for cycling races. But none offer specific guidance on preparing for sportive rides like the Étape.

That's the reason for writing this book. We want to offer specific advice on preparing for sportive rides. We also want to take the latest scientific approaches to training and adapt them to the lifestyles of the ordinary rider. We all have other commitments and have only a limited amount of time to train. But we can all benefit from scientific training advice so that we make the most of the time available. The aim of this book is to help you to fulfil your potential as a sportive rider. In the words of Chris Boardman, Olympic pursuit champion and a winner of three Tour de France stages, the aim of any athlete is to 'be the best that they can be'.

In any race there will be other riders better than you due to their natural ability. Sadly, nothing can be done to change your genetic code! But, with the advice in this book, you should be able to realise your potential. The aim is to get you to the start line in the sportive of your choice, knowing that you are in the best shape and as well prepared as it is possible for you to be. If you cross the finish line and say to yourself 'I couldn't have done any better today' then this book will have served its purpose.

There are, of course, many reasons why people take up the challenge of sportive riding. For some, the desire to ride the Étape du Tour comes from watching the Tour de France. But if you were to ask riders on the start line of any sportive why they are doing it, you would get a myriad of different answers. It may be just the challenge of it, a desire to prove something to yourself or a way of motivating yourself to get fit or lose weight.

Whatever your goal, there is something in this book to help you achieve it. Much of the advice given here builds on the experience of Dr Garry Palmer with Sportstest clients, who take part in a range of endurance sports including cycling, running and triathlon. Sportstest has also carried out physiological testing at English Premier League football clubs and on Formula One racing drivers. This work not only involves giving expert advice and training feedback to elite competitors; the same level of expertise is offered to club competitors who want to realise their potential. Many Sportstest clients have the additional goal of wanting to lose weight. Often they are people in their forties or fifties who have found it difficult to get back in shape despite putting a lot of effort into training. Many of these riders find that, although they may be clocking up hundreds of miles a week on the bike, the weight just won't come off. After a consultation, they quickly realise that it is their dietary habits that are letting them down and, with a bit of expert advice, they are soon shedding those extra pounds.

This book is meant to be a 'one-stop shop' for anyone riding sportives and for whatever reason. Each section focuses on a particular aspect of preparation, but some sections may be more relevant to you than others. For example, if you are cycling to lose weight, the nutrition chapter may be more important to you than the sections on training.

While we have focused most of our attention on sportives because of the boom in their popularity, the information can easily be adapted to suit most endurance cycling disciplines, be it road racing, time trialling, participation in audax events and randonnées, or even if you are looking to tackle a charity cycling event.

Tools for the job

It is important to remember, however, that the advice in this book is based on a holistic approach. As such, it's difficult to make sense of the nutritional advice unless you know how it relates to the physiological effects of training. It's worth taking a little time to get to grips with the training principles first before moving on to advice on nutrition, the importance of recovery and so on.

The better you understand the principles involved, the more likely you are to stick with the training when it gets tough. We see little point in asking you to do something without explaining why. We're sure there are many cyclists, and we have been guilty of this ourselves in the past, who have been out training and found themselves wondering, 'Is this actually doing me any good?'

It is a thought guaranteed to sap anyone's strength and willpower. After reading this book we want you to be out on your bike knowing exactly what you are doing and why you are doing it. We want you to understand how your body works, how it responds to training and how to fine-tune it to the demands of the challenge you have set yourself.

We want you to become your own coach, and in this book you will be given the knowledge to do just that. In these pages are all the tools you need. We will leave you to finish the job.

2

MORE THAN JUST SPORTIVES

History of sportives

Sportive riding has been around for a long time, but it is only in the last 15 years or so that it has become so popular that thousands of riders travel from all parts of the globe to compete in events. In the early years of the Tour de France it was possible to take part as a *touriste-routier*. Up until 1938 all you had to do was find your own accommodation and, as long as you abided by the rules, you were in the Tour de France (though you would most probably find yourself way behind more professional riders who had helpers to support them). This was a form of sportive riding, as the *touriste-routiers* were riding on the same roads as the star riders, though most were not at the same level competitively.

Sportive riding as we know it today began with the increase in popularity of the Étape du Tour and Gran Fondo events in Italy. The setting up of

sports travel firms that offered packages to such events made it more feasible for cyclists to consider travelling from abroad to do these rides. The popularity of the Étape in the 1990s really kick-started the upsurge in interest in sportives, and was itself a consequence of the globalisation of the Tour de France from the 1980s onwards.

It was only in the 1980s that the Tour began to become a truly worldwide sporting event. In the 1970s most of the riders were from continental Europe, with only a handful of English-speaking competitors. This limited the race's appeal to international television; there was little incentive for American or Australian TV networks to cover a race that had no riders from those countries.

In the 1980s that all changed, with more riders from the UK, United States and Australia taking part. The French Peugeot squad had what became known as the 'Foreign Legion', with Englishmen Sean Yates and Graham Jones, Scotland's Robert Millar, Australia's Allan Peiper and Phil Anderson and Ireland's Stephen Roche. Then in the mid-1980s came the Colombians, who dominated the mountain stages. American Greg Lemond became the first English-speaking Tour winner in 1986. And the 7-Eleven pro team became the first US-based team to compete. In later years riders arrived from Eastern Europe.

All of this helped to make the Tour a truly global event and broke the stranglehold of continental Europeans. The organisers came to embrace the foreign influence and welcomed more and more overseas riders as part of a process called 'mondialisation' – making the Tour one of the world's leading sports events.

Today, despite its controversies in recent years, it is the biggest annual sporting event in the world. Only the Olympic Games and football's World Cup attract a larger TV audience. The Tour is watched by a larger live audience than any other sporting event, with some 15 million people standing at the roadside to cheer on the riders. Its massive appeal has inspired countless people to take up cycling, many of whom have been drawn to the Étape du Tour to try to sample for themselves what it is like to ride a stage in the world's greatest bike race.

The Étape has created a snowball effect, with event organisers in other countries creating their own sportive rides ideal for those training for the Étape. International sportives are celebrations of cycling, where riders from all over the world can come together to share their passion for the sport.

Ultra-endurance events

A gruelling, long-distance cycling event lasting one day may be enough for most people, but there are events out there to satisfy those who want something even more challenging. Riding day after day is a severe test of your stamina and powers of recovery. But such events can be incredibly rewarding, so we have picked out two of the most well known.

Land's End to John O'Groats (End to End)

This is not strictly a sportive ride, because there is no mass-start Land's End to John O'Groats event. But it is a popular challenge ride from the southernmost point of England to the northernmost point of Scotland (or vice versa). Some travel firms offer 10- or 14-day packages, with cyclists left to concentrate on riding while their luggage is transferred between hotels after each day's 'stage'. It's around 1400 km (880 miles) and official record attempts are made from time to time. For the record, the fastest time recorded was by English cyclist Andy Wilkinson, who took just 41 hours. Co-author Garry Palmer did the route as a 17-year-old, taking seven days to complete it. Not bad, but he's got a lot of training to do to get that record!

Figure 2.1 Garry (left) with riding partner Stuart Cruikshank, having completed the End to End ride

Race Across America (RAAM)

Again, this is not a sportive ride but it is a big target for many endurance cyclists. Outside of the Tour de France, the Race Across America is considered by many to be the ultimate test. The RAAM, however, is a prestigious race in its own right and its origins can be traced back to the 1880s, when newspaper man George Nellis crossed America on his single-speed bike following railroad tracks. It was, perhaps, appropriate that he was following the railway because his iron bike weighed only slightly less than a locomotive, tipping the scales at 20.5 kg (45 lb)!

Nellis set a record of 80 days for the crossing. After his pioneering ride, others were inspired to take up the challenge and the record was gradually reduced, with times being cut dramatically as roads, bikes and training methods improved.

In the late 1970s two riders emerged who set about smashing the record for a coast-to-coast ride. John Marino and Michael Shermer trained together in California and hatched a plan to make the crossing a race rather than just a series of individual record attempts. They founded the Ultra Marathon Cycling Association and in 1982 organised the Great American Bike Race. A year later the event became the Race Across America and one of the greatest challenges on two wheels was born.

Today the Race Across America attracts entrants from all over the world for both solo and team events, which run from Oceanside in California to Atlantic City in New Jersey. The route is 4800 km, with more than 30,000 metres of climbing (98,525 feet)! Team events are run on a relay basis, with one rider on the road at all times. Currently, the fastest time recorded for a solo rider is by Pete Penseyres in 1986. He took just 8 days, 9 hours and 47 seconds to complete the race, which is an average speed of 24.78 km/h (15.4 mph).

If you are thinking about taking on the challenge of the RAAM, you will have to complete qualifying events before being accepted.

For teams of up to six riders, there is also a 24-hour corporate challenge comprising the first part of the course – around 725 km (450 miles). In team races covering the entire route, an elite male squad of four will average around 38 km/h (24 mph) for the entire race, so the standards set are very high. To complete the race comfortably within the time limit, RAAM veterans recommend that a male team of four should each be able to complete a century ride – 160 km (100 miles) in five and a half hours. If all four members of the team can complete such a ride they should, barring illness or injury, be able to complete the RAAM. There are competitions for mixed teams, tandems and a host of other categories based on age and experience. It's a massive test not just of aerobic endurance, but also of a rider's powers of recovery and mental determination.

Apart from the distance and time covered by the RAAM, the main thing that makes it different to other sportive-type events is the need to have a support crew. This is a requirement of entry into the race and teams or solo riders will need to have an organised and willing team around them if they are to go the distance.

Another consideration is the prospect of night riding and of riding when deprived of sleep. Elite solo riders can get by with as little as four hours' sleep per day. The combination of lack of sleep, fatigue and dehydration is a potentially lethal cocktail because it affects concentration and bike handling. It can prove too much for even the most experienced endurance riders.

The RAAM also attracts ex-pros, including Jonathan Boyer, the first American ever to compete in the Tour de France in 1981. During his pro career, mostly with the 7-Eleven team, Boyer completed the Tour de France five times, managing to finish twelfth overall in 1983. Now in his fifties, Boyer has won races in several RAAM categories, including victory in the 50+ class in 2006. Boyer is one of the few riders to have ridden both the Tour de France and the RAAM, so he is an ideal man to ask which is the tougher. He is in no doubt that the Tour de France is harder for, although it is shorter, the race is run at a much higher average speed. The Tour also attracts all of the world's best endurance riders whereas the RAAM, although it has a top-class field every year, does not pull in the cream of pro cycling.

But the RAAM is a great event in its own right and it does have something that the Tour de France will never have. The Tour is limited to 180 or so of the world's best pro riders; amateur riders are not allowed in no matter how enthusiastic they are. And that's where the RAAM has an edge: it is a race of Tour de France proportions that is open to almost anyone if they reach a certain standard. It is a Tour de France for the people, not just an elite few.

So the RAAM may not quite have the stature of the Tour de France, but it is more accessible and in that sense more democratic. But then America is the land of the free, so it is fitting that the nation's greatest bike race should offer a chance for everyone to race and share the glory.

For more information about the RAAM, go to www.raceacrossamerica.org.

Audax rides and randonnées

Audax rides and randonnées are two more popular long-distance events. They are non-competitive; the challenge is just to get to the finish, stopping off at checkpoints along the way. Indeed audax rides have a *maximum* permissible speed, so if you get to a checkpoint too early you may find that it's not set up and you have to wait! Usually the controls are cafés or other places where you can rest and eat.

Each entrant is given a detailed description of the route, but is otherwise left to complete the distance unassisted. The rider is free to set their own pace, just as long as their overall average speed stays between the minimum and maximum specified for the event. At the start you get a card, which has to be filled in at each control, to show that the course has been completed.

Audax events are popular because you don't have to be a super-fit racer to ride, but you do need to be able to maintain your own steady touring speed for several hours. Many sportive riders will also use audax events as long training sessions, or as a stepping stone to more competitive events they may be planning, but with the knowledge that there will be others riding the same route, and friendly help on hand if they get into difficulties.

These events tend to have no speed limit and riders are allowed to go at their own pace,

although the events are still not strictly races. But both audax events and randonnées can be a great way of getting in some steady training miles and are ideal for discovering new routes.

The word 'audax' originates from the Latin word for courageous and in the latter part of the nineteenth century there were groups of cyclists around Europe who became known as 'les Audacieux' after organising long-distance rides. In 1904 Henri Desgrange, the father of the Tour de France, developed an audax style of riding. It consisted of a group of cyclists riding with a leader setting the pace. While this style is still a widespread feature of European cycling, it is much less popular than the randonnée, which later developed into individual long-distance touring-style cycling.

Probably one of the most prestigious events in the international audax calendar is the 1200 km (745 miles) Paris–Brest–Paris (PBP). This is no longer held in a 'race' format, but it still takes place every four years and is one of the highlights of the European calendar for long-distance riders. In order to participate in the PBP, riders need to have completed several rides up to and including a 600km event in the same year of entry, so the PBP is not for the faint-hearted!

Charity events

If a sportive, audax, randonnée, or ultra-distance ride seem a little daunting, a charity ride may be a sensible way to 'test the waters'. Many people take up cycling after getting involved in charity bike rides. Whether it's a few kilometres, a 250 km (155 miles) epic mountain ride, or a tour in far-flung places, it can be the start of a new passion for cycle sport as a way to keep fit or to experience the thrill of racing.

Charity riders can gain just as much from this book as more experienced riders who are aiming to improve their performance in races. Just because you have never trained seriously for a cycling event before doesn't mean that you should ignore the benefits of training scientifically.

If a charity ride motivates you to do more cycling events, it's sensible to start training properly right from the word go. By doing so, you will make more rapid progress and avoid some of the mistakes made by many people new to cycling. If your fitness improves rapidly, and you avoid

illness and injury caused by overtraining, you will have more fun and want to ride even more. So it makes sense to start as you mean to go on.

There are thousands of charity rides to choose from all around the world. Whether they are week-long tours on mountain bikes or single-day road rides, they all offer a challenge – and you have the added motivation of knowing that it is all in a good cause. If long-distance cycling is a new adventure for you, you may find the idea of riding hundreds of kilometres daunting at first. That's why a charity ride is a good place to start; the thought of raising money for a worthwhile cause gives you something to focus on when the training gets tough. Also, the thought of our friends making fun of us if we quit can make us all find the motivation to get out and do that four-hour training ride in the rain!

3

THE ÉTAPE DU TOUR: THE DADDY OF ALL SPORTIVES

Sportive riding is now a global sport in itself. There are hundreds of events to choose from, so you can find one near you or travel to one of the big international events. We will highlight some of the biggest and best organised events, but there are many, many more out there for you to discover. There really is only one place to start our ride guide and that's the Étape du Tour, the daddy of all sportive rides.

The Étape du Tour

The event began in 1993 to accommodate the massive number of cycling fans who wanted to ride a mountain stage of the Tour de France. Over the years the race has included almost all of the classic *cols* in the Tour. Alpe d'Huez, the Tourmalet and Mont Ventoux have all featured in the Étape. The field is limited to around 8,500 riders and it doesn't take long for the entries to be filled when the route is announced in the

autumn. No Étape du Tour is easy, just as no mountain stage of the Tour de France is easy.

There are probably tougher sportives around, but no other event has the prestige, history and romance of the Étape. For many riders there's nothing better than racing over the same roads as their heroes just a few days before the Tour de France tackles the stage for real.

Some package tour companies offer trips to ride the Étape, which is usually held on a rest day in the Tour de France, and then take the riders to see the actual stage being raced a couple of days later. The event is staged by ASO (Amaury Sport Organisation), the body which organises the Tour de France, Paris-Roubaix and Paris-Nice ProTour races. The standard of organisation is unrivalled, with completely closed roads, feed stations, Mavic neutral service vehicles and medical back-up.

The day before the Étape, gold, silver and bronze standards are posted up in the start village. The standards are age-related so everyone has a realistic target to aim for. There are control points along the route and riders of all ages must maintain a minimum average speed and reach these points before the time limit. Failure to do so leads to disqualification and a trip back to the finish in the *voiture balai* (broom wagon)! Time limits vary each year, but as a guide you must be able to maintain an average speed of around 18–19 km/h (11–12 mph) over the whole route. That may not sound much if you have not ridden in the high mountains before, but it requires a good level of fitness and first-timers should respect the challenge that the Étape poses. Each year hundreds of riders are eliminated due to a lack of preparation or a belief that they can amble along in the first few miles and not be disqualified.

The vast majority of the Étape peloton is French, and they have to qualify for the event by completing other sportives. Overseas riders can apply straight to the organisers, but most come via package tours where entry is guaranteed.

Étape profiles

The Étape, like the Tour de France, changes each year. Looking at recent years' races gives an example of how the routes and climbs vary. The profiles listed include the categorised climbs on the routes; that is, those climbs deemed difficult enough by the Tour de France organisers to be listed in the route profile. Tour climbs are categorised from 1 to 4. There are also *hors categorie* (HC) climbs, which are the hardest of all. Categories vary not just because of the climbs themselves, but because of where they are on the stage. So a climb may be a 3 one year if it's early on in a stage, but become a 2 another year if it's late in a stage. The big mountains, though, are always HC or 1. The following stage routes list only the climbs that were categorised each year; there were many other small hills and rises to get over as well.

2002: Aime to Cluses, Haute Savoie, French Alps (142 km/88 miles)

Climbs: Cormet de Roselend, Col des Saisies, Col des Aravis, Col de la Colombière

This route offered hardly a flat road but around 56 km (35 miles) of climbing, with spectacular descents in between each of the four climbs. You may think that a long-distance event like this would start with a gentle roll out as the riders eased into a tough ride in the mountains. But Étapes tend to start fast and this one was exceptionally quick: the first climb began just 6 km (3.7 miles) from the start. The Cormet de Roselend is a long, narrow climb and most riders knew there would be a bottleneck that might delay them, so there was a mad dash to get to the front. As it happened, a police motorbike toppled over on the climb, causing a delay that then left hundreds of riders at a standstill while the bottleneck was sorted out. There is a lesson to be learned here in carefully studying the race profile and working out just how this will affect the early part of the race.

The stage was run in baking temperatures with the mercury hitting 32°C (90°F), and there was no breeze to cool the riders. The Roselend was the longest climb at some 19 km (12 miles), with the summit at 1,968 metres (6,456 feet). The final climb of the Colombière was tough, with a very fast, hazardous descent to the finish. There were several crashes on this descent, even though riders had been warned of the dangers before the race.

2003: Pau to Bayonne, Pyrenees (202 km/125 miles)
Climbs: Col du Soudet, Col de Larrau, Col de Bagargui, Col de Burdincurutcheta

There were 8,500 starters for this one, but only 6,300 got to the finish. The high attrition rate was surprising as this was not considered the hardest mountain stage on that year's Tour route. What caught out lots of riders was the Col de Bagargui, which had many searching for the gears with its sudden steep sections. Riders who were over-geared or simply lacking fitness were frequently reduced to walking; this resulted in them losing so much time that they were eliminated. After the final categorised climb of the Burdincurutcheta with around 80 km (50 miles) remaining, many riders thought that the rest of the route was more or less flat. UK cycling magazines had done profiles of the route and suggested that the last 80 km (50 miles) were easy, but the reality was a little different. It was an undulating route, made more difficult by riders facing a headwind and being fatigued from the tough climbs earlier in the ride.

Former pro riders competing included five-time Tour de France winner Miguel Indurain and former ONCE pro and Tour stage winner Abraham Olano. Also in the field was former Formula One motor racing champion Alain Prost.

2004: Limoges to St Flour, Massif Central (239 km/148 miles)
Climbs: Col de Lestards, Col de Néronne, Col de Pas de Peyrol, Col d'Entremont and the Plomb du Cantal

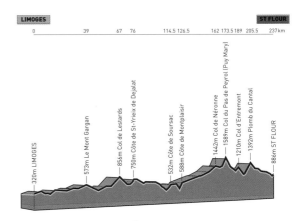

Figure 3.1 The route of the Étape in 2004

This was, and is at the time of writing, the longest stage ever used for the Étape du Tour. It was also the longest stage of that year's Tour de France. As the co-author of this book Richard Allen remembers only too well, it was a hard, hard ride. The weather was perfect: overcast and cool with little wind. However, the distance – and having to tackle one climb after another with undulating, heavy roads in between – was a tough test. Due to the length of the stage, organisers were keen to get the peloton away from the start as quickly as possible, so some riders had to get up at 4 am to get breakfast and make their way through the crowds for a 6.30 am start. The organisers also wanted a quick start to the stage so that they could begin reopening the roads around Limoges. This meant an early checkpoint was put in at around 30 km (18 miles) and some riders who took it too easy in the opening kilometres found themselves bundled into the broom wagon before the race had really begun!

Most of the climbs were not particularly steep and were just long, steady ascents. The exception was the Pas de Peyrol after around 160 km (100 miles), which had a steep section of around 15 to 20 per cent. This caught out a lot of competitors at the back of the field, who quickly went from being cyclists to pedestrians.

It was on this part of the course that the Tour de France stage was decided. As it was Bastille Day, it was expected that French riders would go on the attack and Richard Virenque set the race alight. He broke clear with Axel Merckx after around 30 km (19 miles) and, on the climb of the Pas de Peyrol, broke clear from Merckx and rode alone to the finish.

By the time the Étape riders had ridden back to their hotels at the end of the day, they had clocked up more than 250 km (155 miles). For many, it would have been the longest they had ever spent on a bike.

In the 2004 field were Abraham Olano, Alain Prost and former Wimbledon tennis champion Richard Krajicek. The Étape was won by Jean-Christophe Currit, who covered the 239 km (148 miles) in 6 hours 57 minutes. A few days later in the Tour de France, the stage winner Richard Virenque covered the same route in 6 hours and 24 seconds.

2005: Mourenx to Pau, Pyrenees (179 km/ 111 miles)

Climbs – Col d'Ichère, Col de Marie-Blanque, Col d'Aubisque, Col du Soulor

After the previous year's ultra-marathon, the organisers seemed to take pity on the Etapists with this relatively short stage. It was still demanding though, the major challenge being the Col d'Aubisque with its summit at 1,677 metres (5,501 feet), the high point of the stage. Of the 8,500 starters, some 2,500 were from outside France, emphasising the international appeal of the event. Some 7,200 riders finished. The Étape winner was Laurent Marcon in 5 hours 22 minutes. In the Tour de France stage, eventual race-winner Oscar Pereiro took the honours in 4 hours 38 minutes.

2006: Gap to Alpe d'Huez (193 km/120 miles)

Climbs: Col d'Izoard, Col du Lautaret, Alpe d'Huez

The 2006 edition of the Étape was a truly classic stage, with the finish at 'The Alp', sacred ground for Tour fanatics. Winning at Alpe d'Huez has made legends out of riders throughout the Tour's history, beginning in 1952 when Fausto Coppi won the first stage ever to feature the mountain. The Izoard is a tough climb at 2,361 metres (7,746 feet) and the Lauraret is not easy either at 2,011 metres (6,957 feet). However Alpe d'Huez is harder than both, even though its summit is lower at 1,860 metres (6,102 feet). This is because it comes at the end of a stage and, with an average gradient of 8 per cent, offers little chance to recover if you go too far into the red zone.

There are 21 numbered hairpin bends, which play on the mind because each bend seems to pass more slowly than the previous one. The hairpin bends also carry the names of riders who have won stages on the mountain. The Étape winner in 2006 was Blaise Sonnery in 6 hours 33 seconds. Frank Schleck won the Tour de France stage over the same route in 4 hours 52 minutes. Interestingly, especially for those of us who watch the Tour de France and go on about the sprinters not being able to climb, the last finisher on the Tour de France stage was faster than the winner of the Étape du Tour.

2007: Foix to Loudenville, Pyrenees (196 km/122 miles)
Climbs: Col de Port, Col de Portet d'Aspet, Col de Mente, Port de Bales, Col de Peyresourde

No climbs over 2,000 metres (6,561 feet) but five categorised ascents made this a true test for Étapists and Tour de France competitors alike. Climbing the *cols* amounted to a total of 4,400 metres (14,435 feet). That's about half of the total height of Mount Everest. It gives you some idea of the scale of the task involved in completing the Étape. The Col de

Mente, which began at around 100 km (62 miles) into the route, has the steepest average gradient at 8.1 per cent. But the hardest climb was saved for last, the brutal Peyresoude at 10 km (6 miles) and averaging a gradient of 7.8 per cent.

The Étape was won by ex-pro rider Nicolas Fritsche, who had completed the Tour de France in 2003. He crossed the finish line in 6 hours 21 minutes. In the Tour de France proper, this stage was won by Alexandre Vinokourov in 5 hours 34 minutes, although he was later ejected from the race after failing a drugs test. On the descent of the Portet d'Aspet, all of the riders — Étapists and Tour de France elite alike — were reminded of the dangers of riding in the high mountains. A wing-wheeled statue marks the spot where former Olympic champion Fabio Casartelli died after crashing into a concrete bollard in the 1995 Tour de France: a reminder to all cyclists that the challenge they set themselves deserves respect.

2008: Pau to Hautacam (189 km/117 miles)
Climbs: Col du Tourmalet, Hautacam

Although the Hautacam was regarded by Lance Armstrong as one of the Tour's toughest climbs, at the time of writing, this stage appears to be one of the easiest in recent years. The Tourmalet and Hautacam are hard climbs, but with only two major ascents on the route it appears that the organisers are maybe hoping to increase the percentage of riders making the finish within the time limit.

CONQUERING CANCER

'I now have only good days and great days.' Lance Armstrong

A 50/50 chance. That's all Steve Timmins was given when he was diagnosed with bowel cancer in February 2001.

At the time he was an accomplished club racer, attaining the level of a second category rider in the UK. After an operation and a lengthy period of chemotherapy, Steve began reading Lance Armstrong's autobiography *It's Not About the Bike* and found it to be an inspiration.

'I just couldn't put the book down,' remembers Steve. 'I read that he went out training during his chemotherapy and I was told a little exercise would be okay for me. So I went out cycling with my daughter. When I was first diagnosed, I thought I would have to give up cycling, but that was the least of my worries at the time. Armstrong's story made me believe that I could try to regain my fitness.'

Figure 3.2 Steve Timmins has completed the entire Tour de France route to raise money for a cancer charity and has ridden the Étape du Tour three times

Steve certainly did that. He rode the Étape du Tour in 2003, just over two years after he was first diagnosed, and raised money for the Bobby Moore Cancer Fund. Steve was hoping to improve on his previous performance in the race, which at 238 km (148 miles) was not only the longest stage of that year's Tour de France but also the longest stage in the history of the Étape du Tour. Garry Palmer helped him prepare for the 2004 Étape for just eight weeks before the race and, despite the short time frame, Steve made surprisingly rapid improvements between tests.

Steve struggled with a recurrence of an old knee injury on the day of the Étape but still managed a silver medal, just missing gold by 10 minutes. He found Garry's advice invaluable in preparing for the event: 'Garry helped me train for the Étape by introducing me properly to the scientific method of training using heart rate zones,' says Steve. 'When he looked at the training I had been doing previously, it was clear that much of it was in the dead zone between two training levels. My riding had been too intense for an endurance ride but not intense enough to gain any benefits from riding shorter, faster efforts in the threshold zone. But with the training programme, my training was specific to the demands of the Étape. 'Working nine to five, I was unable to get many long rides in to prepare for a 238 km (148 miles) race. But the programme allowed for this, with just Sunday set aside for a long-distance ride. Garry also taught me how to hydrate properly and eat sufficiently for an event as demanding as the Étape.'

TAKING ON THE TOUR

After tackling the Étape, Steve was back to full fitness and had renewed his enthusiasm for the sport. Doing the Étape is a major achievement for any rider, especially someone who has fought back against cancer. But Steve had much bigger fish to fry and in 2007 he was part of a team of cancer survivors who cycled the route of the Tour de France to raise money for charity. The team was led by former England international footballer Geoff Thomas. Thomas had ridden the route previously after recovering from leukaemia, but this was Steve's first attempt at riding a three-week tour.

'Being asked to ride the Tour de France route by Geoff Thomas gave me the opportunity to test myself, to see if I was up to emulating the pros by riding 3,550 km (2,205 miles) in 21 days,' says Steve. 'The day before the Tour started, the Geoff Thomas Foundation – Team Unity – was asked to take part in the official Tour de France team presentation being held in Trafalgar Square in London. To be introduced to the crowds, estimated at 250,000, before the pro teams was a real buzz and something that will stay with me for the rest of my life.

Having never done back-to-back 100 mile rides before, the prospect of starting with eight consecutive rides between 177 and 233 km (110 and 145 miles) was daunting. 'It was probably the toughest part mentally as I was waiting for the mountains to appear. After the first week I seemed to get into a routine and the distances didn't seem to hurt as my system adapted to the strain placed upon it. The mountains of the Alps and Pyrenees are just brutal; you can see why cycling fans love to watch their heroes struggling up them. For me the Tour is all about the mountains as you test yourself, man against gradient, beautiful yet hostile, painful yet a feeling of euphoria as you crest the top. It's a feeling you have to experience at least once in your life.

'Riding a cyclosportive is hard, but doing Le Tour takes it to another level as you have to get up the following day and do it all again, then again and again. This leads to fatigue, and aches and pains start. I developed sore fingers and wrists for the last three days. I had a sore and swollen knee for the first two and a half weeks. A new bike, shoes, cleats and pedals two weeks before an event like this are most certainly *not* recommended. My overriding memory was the spirit within the team, riders and support staff. If anyone was struggling, there was always someone to drop back and encourage or pace you back.

'At first it was polite handshakes and congratulations at the finish, but within no time these were replaced by high fives and hugs of congratulation as the bonding process took hold. I probably did fewer miles than anyone else on the team in training, only having Sundays to do a long ride. Garry insisted this would not be a problem and the programme they set me more than made up for the lack of regular long mileage. It brought me to the start with my fitness in great shape, and well rested.'

Steve's experience just goes to show that more training is not necessarily an advantage.

More information about the Geoff Thomas Foundation can be found at www.geoffthomasfoundation.com.

Étape de Légende

This event is run on the same principle as the Étape du Tour and is also organised by ASO. The difference from the Étape du Tour being that the route is one from a historic Tour de France stage.

The event began in autumn 2007 with the 210 km (130 miles) stage of the Pyrenees. Originally used in the Tour in 1967, and won by Lucien Aimar, the route included six climbs in the Vosges mountains, with a tough 10 km (6 miles) ascent to the finish line. Some 3,000 riders took part in the event. The historic dimension appeals to many because it allows them to ride the routes of famous stages they may have watched on TV when being inspired to take up cycling.

4

THE UCI GOLDEN BIKE SERIES

While many aspiring sportive riders will dream of following in the footsteps of the pros and aim to complete the Étape, the UCI Golden Bike series is also well worth considering. These are events granted quality status by the UCI (Union Cycliste Internationale), cycling's international governing body.

The UCI regards these events as the best organised in the world. To gain Golden Bike status, organisers have to adhere to strict terms and conditions, in particular rules governing overseas participants. Currently there are nine UCI Golden Bike events in nine different countries (dates correct at time of publication):

- Cape Argus Pick 'n' Pay Cycle Tour – South Africa (March)

- Tour of Flanders (Ronde van Vlaanderen) – Belgium (April)
- Toerversie Amstel Gold Race – Holland (April)
- Gran Fondo Internazionale Felice Gimondi – Italy (May)
- Quebrantahuesos – Spain (June)
- Cyclosportive l'Ariégeoise – France (June)
- Gruyère Cycling Tour – Switzerland (August)
- Rothaus RiderMan – Germany (September)
- Wattyl Lake Taupo Cycle Challenge – New Zealand (November)

Cape Argus Pick 'n' Pay Cycle Tour
More than 35,000 riders tackle this sportive each year around Cape Town. It's the biggest mass participation ride in the world. Not a particularly testing route covering just 105 km (65 miles), with the elites finishing in less than 2 hours

40 minutes, the thrill of this ride is being part of a carnival atmosphere. The Argus takes place each March in the majestic surroundings of the Cape Peninsula. Its route skirts both the Indian and Atlantic oceans, but most memorable is probably riding the spectacular Chapman's Peak Drive. This 4 km (2.5 miles) winding climb (reported to have 114 corners over its 9 km (5.5 miles) length) has been the location for many a motoring advert and offers some stunning views of Hout Bay as the riders head back towards the finish in Camps Bay.

Sportstest used riders in the pro race of the 1993 Argus to produce the first ever scientific document about the physiological responses recorded during actual cycle competition. The results of our investigations showed that, despite an average racing speed of 40.6 ± 0.5 km/h (25.2 ± 0.3mph), the heart rate responses of the elite riders were, as is shown in Figure 4.1, random in frequency and amplitude. They also demonstrate that the athletes were performing at a relatively low intensity. In fact, the average heart rate for the entire race was 151 ± 17 beats per minute (78.6 ± 8.9 % of maximum heart rate, which corresponded to approximately 66% of VO_2max).

The key to the investigation was interpretation of the heart rate responses of these riders. As can be seen, the heart rate response (top, right) *appears* to mirror the course profile (bottom, right) such that any increase in gradient is accompanied by an increase in heart rate and vice versa. Although it is tempting to speculate that this stochastic physiological response is merely a reflection of, and directly related to, the terrain of the course, closer examination of the data reveals that this is not the

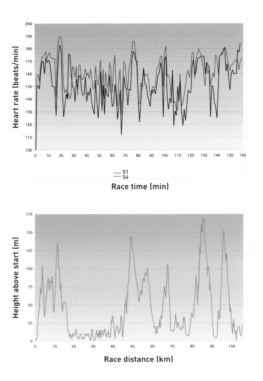

Figure 4.1 Samples of elite riders' physiological responses during the 1993 Argus (upper panel) and the profile of the route (lower panel). Data reproduced from Palmer G., et al.: Medicine and Science in Sport and Exercise 26 (10), 1994

case. For example, during a relatively flat section of the Argus, which occurs between 20 km (12.5 miles) and 40 km (25 miles), the heart rate responses of the cyclists remained highly variable, albeit slightly lower, despite the lack of perturbations in the course. This suggests that the major factor responsible for the stochastic nature of the heart rate responses in mass-start races is not the course profile per se, but is rather a result of the group dynamics of the cyclists. These findings have impacted on the training regimens that we offer.

You can find out more about the Argus at www.cycletour.co.za.

AN AFRICAN EXPERIENCE: THE CAPE ARGUS PICK 'N' PAY TOUR

Riding with 35,000 cyclists in South Africa's Cape Argus Pick 'n' Pay Cycle Tour is an experience Jo Wright will never forget. The 47-year-old construction project manager was an experienced sportive rider before she took part in the Argus, but it was different from any other ride she had experienced.

She first heard about the Argus after reading a feature in *Pro Cycling* magazine. Inspired by the stunning pictures of the biggest peloton in any bike ride anywhere in the world, she decided it was to be her next challenge. As it is in March and not too taxing at around 105 km (65 miles) and relatively flat, Jo felt that it was an ideal ride for the time of year and good early season preparation for a tougher sportive ride in June or July. 'If you are aiming to do the Étape du Tour in July, you don't want to be peaking too early in the year,' she says. 'The distance isn't going to kill you, even that early in the year. It's a good, classic opening event to do if you can afford to go there.'

The other advantage of doing the Argus, especially if you live in a cold climate like that in northern Europe, is that the South African weather is perfect for cycling around March. Jo, who lives and works in London, had spent much of the winter on her turbo trainer to escape England's cold and wet climate. She also supplemented her training by riding to work on her fixed-gear bike and using these as recovery rides. Longer rides were done with friends at the weekend. 'The weather at the Argus made a real difference after I had been training in cold and wet weather in the winter. Riding in South Africa in the sunshine makes you realise what you are training for in the summer if you are preparing for an event like the Étape du Tour. The race is very well organised, although you have to concentrate all the time because there are so many people on the road.'

PRO RIDERS LEAD THE WAY

Riders start in groups of equal ability at 10-minute intervals, with the first group being a professional race made up of international cyclists. Although organisers warn riders about the severity of the climbs on the course, Jo feels that anyone who has ridden the Étape or a Grand Fondo should not have any problem at all. Jo has ridden the Argus in 2005 and 2007 and has also taken part in the Étape du Tour and in Gran Fondo events in Italy. She says the Argus offers a fantastic atmosphere, with huge crowds turning out to cheer on the riders.

Jo undertook a physiological test at Sportstest with the aim of improving her cycling and she then decided to try some sportive events. To get the most out of the training schedule she was given, Jo felt she had to be quite dedicated and focused. But she found that it didn't take long for the training to start to have an effect.

Jo's physiology made it difficult for her to cope with a high volume of training. She had been advised by a cycling coach to put in a lot of miles when training for the Étape du Tour, resulting in her overtraining. However, the physiological test identified that she needed to do fewer hours on the bike and allow her body more time to recover between hard training sessions to achieve her objective.

Tour of Flanders (Ronde van Vlaanderen)

Belgium is heaven for cyclists and the Tour of Flanders is one of the country's two ProTour events. The sportive ride usually takes place the day before the elite riders tackle the ProTour event. The full race distance is around 260 km (160 miles), but there are usually shorter rides offered too – these are normally about 140 km (87 miles) and 75 km (46 miles). The route is famed for the short but viciously steep cobbled climbs that are dotted around the course. It all starts in Bruges and ends in Meerbeke with around 18,000 riders climbing 18 short steep hills, or *bergs*, many of them cobbled.

Like all road races, the route may change slightly, but the Tour of Flanders will always remain pretty much the same. In 2007 the steepest climb was the Paterberg, coming at 180 km (112 miles). Although only 360 metres (1,181 feet) long, its maximum gradient is 20 per cent and its average 13 per cent. The longest climb was the Oude Kwaremont at 2,200 metres (7,218 feet), averaging 4 per cent in gradient with a maximum of 11.6 per cent. But the hardest climb on the full 259 km (160 miles) route was the second to last. By the time the riders had reached the Muur-Kapelmuur, they already had 240 km (150 miles) hard kilometres in their legs and then faced the 475 metre (1,558 feet) long Muur, with an average gradient of 9.3 per cent and a maximum of 19.8 per cent. Winner of the ProTour event in 2007 was Italian Alessandro Ballan, who covered 259 km (160 miles) in six hours and ten minutes, an average speed of 41.9 km/h (26 mph).

A COBBLED CLASSIC: THE TOUR OF FLANDERS SPORTIVE

Andy Southall is an accomplished sportive rider who has ridden the La Marmotte sportive four times as well as the Tour of Flanders. Andy, aged 42, did the Flanders event in 2006. 'The 140 km (87 miles) route misses out the first 100 km (62 miles) or so, which are relatively flat but that include most of the short, steep climbs used in the pro race,' says Andy, who lives in the English Midlands. Around 18,000 cyclists take part in the sportive rides and you can get held up by a bottleneck of riders on the climb because they are so narrow.'

Andy praised the standard of organisation and was impressed with the feed stations, although it was inevitable that riders had to wait for food due to the sheer volume of people taking part. 'The queue at the first feed station was so long that we just carried on and stopped at a shop to get some food instead. The cobbles on the climb were four inches square with big gaps in between; to make matters worse it had been raining too. On every climb everyone just grinds to a halt and you have to fight your way through the crowd.'

Figure 4.2 Andy Southall

It was a tough test, but Andy says it is an event well worth experiencing. It's also worth hanging around to watch the ProTour race the next day. You can see how the elite riders are able to power up the cobbled climbs on the big chainring as opposed to the 39x25 gear most of the sportive riders use.

Andy has also ridden many UK events including the Fred Whitton ride, which he regards as the toughest event he has tackled. It takes place in the English Lake District, but the riders don't get much chance to admire the scenery. The 177 km (110 miles) route is punctuated by a series of steep climbs, with Hardknott Pass being the toughest (its gradient is 33 per cent).

'The Fred Whitton ride is the hardest I've done in the UK and it's probably harder than the Tour of Flanders because the climbs are just bonkers', says Andy. 'In my opinion some of the climbs are just unrideable if it's wet – they're just so steep. I managed to ride up Hardknott Pass. When I got there, I saw about 50 cyclists on the climb, but there were only about four of us actually riding.'

Before taking up sportive riding Andy had been a keen swimmer and triathlete. He found that the expert physiological tests he undertook helped to target his training to improve aspects of fitness tailored to the specific demands of the event he was preparing for.

Andy also found this approach useful when riding events like La Marmotte. His heart rate targets on long climbs make it easier for him maintain an even pace. Andy says: 'It was a big help to know the level of effort I could sustain on a long climb that may take up to 90 minutes to complete. Getting your pacing right is vital in an event like La Marmotte that features a series of long climbs. If you go too hard on the first climb, you will pay for it later in the day.'

Andy did a lot of training on an iMagic turbo trainer system, which features simulated versions of some of the climbs used in La Marmotte. In training he rode some of the climbs and tried to simulate changes in gradient by altering his gear ratio and pedalling cadence. For example, Alpine climbs tend to be a steady gradient during straight parts, but get steeper on hairpin bends. As he watched the iMagic simulation, Andy would shift to a higher gear and lower cadence as he came up to a hairpin bend and then shift back down as the gradient eased off.

Toerversie Amstel Gold Race

The ProTour Amstel Gold Race began in the 1960s, when it was sponsored by the Amstel brewery. The Toerversie (tour version) of the event takes place before the elite race and is the largest cycling event in Holland. Six different distances are offered to cater for all levels of fitness. Despite its reputation, Holland is *not* flat – as you will find out riding the Amstel, which has a series of short, steep climbs. The race starts in Maastricht and covers 252 km (156 miles) before the finish in Valkenurg. But in between are 31 climbs, which comprise the main difficulty of the race.

There are usually six distances for sportive riders: 50 km (31 miles), 100 km (62 miles), 125 km (77 miles), 150 km (93 miles), 200 km (124 miles) and the full race distance that will also be covered by the elite ProTour riders the next day. On the actual race route, and on the longer sportive routes, some of the climbs will be tackled several times. If you want to compete in this event, get used to riding up climbs from 500 metres (1,640 feet) to around 2 km (1.2 miles) long and with gradients averaging around 10 per cent. Toughest of the climbs is the Cauberg, which appears three times on the full race distance route. It's 1 km long (0.6 miles) and has an average gradient of 10 per cent. Winner of the ProTour race in 2007 was Germany's Stefan Schumacher, who covered the 252.2 km race distance in six hours and eleven minutes, an average speed of 40.6 km/h (25 mph).

Gran Fondo Internazionale Felice Gimondi
Felice Gimondi became a legend of Italian cycling when he won the Tour de France at his first attempt in 1965 at the age of only 22. His professional career spanned 11 years, during which time he won the Giro d'Italia three times and the Tour of Spain. He also had victories in the Tour of Lombardy (twice), Paris-Roubaix and Milan-San Remo. The sportive ride that carries his name is one of the biggest in Italy and regularly attracts many former pro riders. Three distances are offered, ranging from around 100 km to 170 km (62–105 miles).

Quebrantahuesos
Named after a local bird of prey, this is a tough climbing test in the Pyrenées and the largest sportive event in Spain, attracting around 8,000 riders each year. Like the Étape du Tour, the event offers gold, silver and bronze medals depending on your finishing time. Support for the event is similar to the Étape du Tour as it

takes place on closed roads with police patrols on junctions. There are also medical and mechanical support vehicles en route. The 205 km (128 miles) route starts and finishes in Sabinanigo and climbs the Col du Somport, Col du Marie Blanque and the Col du Portalet.

Cyclosportive L'Ariègeoise
Classic Pyrenean climbs used in the Tour de France feature in this sportive in the Ariège region. This is a 163 km (101 miles) event in France, along the Spanish border from Tarascon to Auzat. It attracts around 3,000 riders.

Gruyère Cycling Tour
Switzerland is one of the most beautiful countries in which to ride a bike and the Lac de la Gruyère forms an idyllic backdrop to this event. Three distances are offered, with the longest being around 170 km (105 miles) and taking in the stunning mountain passes around the lake. Shorter routes of 85 km (53 miles) and 125 km (78 miles) are also provided. This event was formerly known as La Pascal Richard sportive ride, named after the former Swiss national champion who was a Tour de France stage winner.

Rothaus RiderMan
This is a sportive event with a difference as it is run like a mini stage race on closed roads. It features a time trial and a road race with distance options. Bad Durrheim in the Black Forest is the starting point for the races, which are a short time trial of 20 km (12 miles) and a circuit road race with options of between 25 km (15.5 miles)

THE ITALIAN EXPERIENCE

Ellis Organ has been to the Étape du Tour three times, successfully completing the event in 2005 and 2006. He did a British sportive ride in 2007 that covered the route of the first road stage of the Tour de France from London to Canterbury.

Ellis also rode the Gran Fondo Campagnolo in 2005, a 212 km (132 miles) route across the Dolomites including four climbs, each with summits of around 2,000 metres (6,561 feet). As an experienced sportive rider, Ellis is a good man to ask about the differences between some of the big European sportive events.

'The Étape and Gran Fondo Campagnolo are equally difficult as they always feature a series of cols. But the standard of riding in the Campagnolo and other Gran Fondos in Italy tends to be of a higher standard than the Étape,' says Ellis, who lives in the Cotswolds. 'The Gran Fondo is definitely a race: it's semi-professional,' he says. 'Most of the Fondos have three different routes on a given day: short, medium and long. If

Figure 4.3 Ellis Organ

you do the long route, it's pretty much a self-selecting group who are very serious about it. Of course, the other thing about Italy is that every little town has its own cycling team.'

PUTTING ON A SHOW

Ellis, aged 44, remembers one section of the Campagnolo ride through a valley between two climbs where one of the local sponsored teams decided to put on a show for their fans. 'There was a group of about 40 of us and one of the local teams got on the front, driving it along at a constant 40 km/h (25 mph).'

This makes the Campagnolo experience even better for overseas riders, who can take full advantage of a train stoked by local pride. 'The standard of descending in the Fondos is higher than in the Étape,' Ellis says. 'Everybody knows what they are doing. What I find on the Étape is that you will be going into a corner catching someone up and they will just change their line without warning. You just don't get that in the Italian ones.'

The Gran Fondo Campagnolo attracts around 4,000 riders. When Ellis failed to complete the 2004 Étape du Tour, he decided to pay more attention to his training regime so that he was better prepared next time.

TRAINING ADVICE

After an initial physiological cycling test, Ellis was given a new training programme that focused on tackling his weaknesses. The training was altered week by week according to the monitored responses. 'I went from not finishing the Étape in 2004 to getting a silver medal the following year,' says Ellis.

Before taking up road biking, Ellis had been a keen mountain biker. But he had never taken a scientific approach to training. Due to his job as director of a corporate finance business, it wasn't easy for him to find the time to train. But having appropriate support, and being realistic about how much time he could devote to his sport, improvements came from then on.

'I sat down with Garry and worked out just how much I could put into it. We worked on a schedule of three days on, one day off, two days on, one day off. Garry set me training blocks of two heavy stress weeks and a medium week, then two heavy weeks and a light week. It was quite demanding, but you could see your endurance and power output going up quite quickly. I was getting up early two mornings a week and training on the turbo with two days a week being a double session, before and after work. I'd do the longer rides at the weekend.'

Ellis also sometimes commutes to work by bike to fit in his training. Working with Sportstest also led Ellis to lose weight, going from 64 kg (141 lb) down to 58 kg (128 lb), which was a big help in improving his climbing ability. Ellis, like many of you out there, has a demanding job and lifestyle. But he has found that, with a bit of thought about training, he is more than capable of finding the time to achieve the cycling goals he has set himself.

and 150 km (93 miles). Run in September, it is an ideal end-of-season event that attracts around 2,000 riders each year.

Wattyl Lake Taupo Cycle Challenge
This New Zealand event offers the challenge of riding the 160 km (100 miles) loop around Lake Taupo. But there are options for individuals and teams. You can enter as a relay team and there are options to do two- or four-lap events – 320 km (200 miles) or 640 km (398 miles). Teams may also choose to do a mountain bike leg at the start of their relay. It is not a competitive event, but there is an elite Classic Race for which entry criteria apply.

A VIEW FROM DOWN UNDER

Having recently emigrated from the UK to New Zealand, Grant Difford undertook the Lake Taupo Cycle Challenge on behalf of his company's charity – the Glen Hyland MS Trust, a charity focused on raising awareness of, and funding for, multiple sclerosis.

This was Grant's first experience of a big sportive and he comments: 'The pre-registration was very simple – all done online and you were sent a race code long before the event. Once at the event, I collected my goody bag with relative ease considering the amount of people taking part. This included bike stickers, numbers, drinks bottles, vouchers, food etc. – pretty much the usual. The event was well catered and in a very spacious venue to create a great warm atmosphere.

'The morning of the race we were split into waves depending on predicted race times.' Grant was in the five hours fifty to six hours ten group. 'I felt really nervous beforehand as

Figure 4.4 Grant Difford

I had only done a maximum ride of 100 km (62 miles) on a fairly flat course; otherwise I was relying on my basic middle-distance training and sheer determination. I started well and wanted to keep a really easy pace so I didn't blow up. I carried 5 litres (8.7 pints) of a water and electrolyte solution in a Camelbak and an additional 2 litres (3.5 pints) of sports drink. I also had three high-energy gels and two energy bars. As it was a busy race, I managed to hook on to the back of a few groups to lift the pace. But I soon found that I was the one doing all the work, especially on the hills, where I seemed to be really strong compared to the flats.

'The course was extremely hilly, which made finding your rhythm really troublesome. I felt strong until 120 km (75 miles), which was what I expected. But then I started to suffer terrible back pain due to the lack of long rides. This caused me to stop every now and then to stretch and rest. The course was littered with support and marshals who were loud and very supportive. I even heard some marshals at points offer to hold people's bikes while they rested, along with offering a lot of refreshments and nutrition.

'The last 40 km (25 miles) was as flat as a pancake and wind-free, but by then I was seriously fatigued and in a lot of pain. I managed to keep a really solid 27 km/h (17mph) pace, which was as planned. Crossing the finish line in five hours, 56 minutes, and 57 seconds was a great feeling; the toughest ride I had ever done. I generally felt great, my legs felt fresh, but my back just ruined me. Extra core strength was really needed!

'After the event we had a corporate tent, so we sat back and enjoyed the atmosphere. At six o'clock there was a huge prize draw for all those who took part and, from what I could tell, all 17,000 riders came back for it. There was also live music and entertainment, and it gave it a real festival atmosphere.

'All in all, it was an amazing event that created a lot of income for many charities and also pushed people to unknown limits. Will I be back next year? Well yes, and I will be focused on getting under five hours!'

Other classic sportives

La Marmotte

Considered by many to be the toughest sportive ride in the world, this event is a challenge even for experienced riders. It is a 174 km (108) ride based in the French Alps that offers a chance to tackle some of the classic cols used in the Tour de France. The Col de la Croix de Fer, Col du Télégraphe, Col du Galibier and a finish at the top of Alpe d'Huez make for a long, hard day. La Marmotte is usually run on a weekend with the following day set aside for the Grimpe L'Alpe d'Huez, a mass start ride from Bourg d'Oisans to the ski station at the top of the mountain made famous by numerous epic battles in the Tour.

There are, of course, many other sportives. Some with vast international appeal like many of the Italian Grand Fondos, or others with small fields, which cater to mainly local entrants. This book cannot replace the wealth of local information about such events, much of which is accessible through the internet. Therefore, we recommend that you look at some of the internet resources we have provided at the end of this book, and find the event that best meets your aims and ambitions.

The pro's experience: a comparison

Some pro riders like Miguel Indurain and Greg Lemond turn out in sportive rides after they have retired from racing. It's a way for them to recapture some of the magic of their glory days, and it gives the average riders alongside them something to tell their grandchildren about!

But some pro riders find that they want to make a comeback and race at a high level many years after their careers have ended. One such rider is Malcolm Elliott, who made a spectacular return to racing at the age of 42. Sportive riding obviously wasn't enough to satisfy his competitive instincts, but his story is interesting for all of those riders returning to the sport in later life.

A 'MASTER' RETURNS

Malcolm Elliott is one of Britain's greatest ever cyclists. Winning the points jersey in the Tour of Spain was the highlight of a glittering career. Having retired in the 1990s, he decided to return to racing in 2003 at the age of 42.

In 2006 he won the British National Circuit Race title and the World Masters Road Race championship. It was a marvellous season and Elliott had planned his training with a little help from us. We carried out a full physiological assessment on the Kingcycle apparatus and the resulting data enabled Elliott to focus his training.

Figure 4.5 Malcolm Elliott, Pinarello RT pro rider and winner of the Tour of Spain sprinters' jersey

During his earlier career, Elliott had raced for Raleigh, ANC-Halfords and the Spanish-based Teka squad. As well as stage wins in the Tour of Spain and the points jersey in that race, he also notched up wins in the Milk Race, Kellogg's Tour of Britain and picked up a fourth place in the Amstel Gold classic. Add to this two Commonwealth gold medals and two finishes in the Tour de France and it is an impressive palmares (a cycling term for a rider's CV of race wins).

However, training back in the 1980s and 90s, even for the world's top riders like Malcolm, did not involve much in the way of scientific testing. Malcolm says that before his visit to us in 2005 he had only undergone similar tests on two other occasions, the last being at Loughborough University in 1984 when he was racing for Raleigh's GB-based pro team.

THE COMEBACK KING

'In all those years as a professional you were really left to your own devices as far as how you got yourself into shape,' Elliott says. 'Since my comeback in 2003 I had really been doing things just by feel and from experience. Things have moved on drastically since I began racing first time round. Although I don't consider myself as someone at the forefront of new technology and new ideas, I did think that I needed to get assessed in a proper, modern way, to see what that identified and work out how to improve. I think everyone can benefit from having a bit more information and expert advice. The test gave me proper parameters to train in and allowed me to see exactly how hard I was working. It's one of the pieces of the jigsaw you need to be able to work on any weak areas. You need that information.'

Despite a successful career spanning a decade, Elliott altered his training when he made his comeback. He now takes a more modern, scientific approach. In the 1980s and 90s most pro riders did smaller races to get fit for more important events. They raced to train; now riders train to race. 'Training is all on my own now,' he says. 'I work substantially harder than I did, but I enjoy it more. Before, when I used to train with others, it was something that I relied on to motivate me to go training, whereas now I can ride exactly as I want at the time that I want.'

Early season training for Malcolm involves four- to five-hour rides four times a week, and 'filling in' with two-three hour rides on other days. In 2007, at the age of 46, Elliott was still competing in elite races in the UK's Premier Calendar series – and still winning. He won the 2007 edition of the East Midlands CiCle Classic, billed as a British version of Paris-Roubaix because it included tough off-road sections across farmland.

Even though he was up against elite young riders, the veteran still came out on top. Many riders return to racing in later life, and many club riders take up the challenge of sportive riding in their forties after family and work commitments have forced them to stop racing in their younger days.

Elliott's return to the sport is, of course, different to the average club rider. He was, in the opinion of many experts, one of Britain's most talented road riders. But his story shows that times have changed, that modern sports science has proven that it can offer better ways to train, ways that take some of the guesswork out of race preparation. Elliot was always a winner, but he was also someone who was prepared to move with the times when he made a comeback to racing.

For those of you making a return to the sport after a long lay-off, it's worth thinking about how you used to train and whether you should consider dropping any old thinking behind your current training regime. We are not suggesting that you go out and try to pack in as much training as Elliott and other pros do. Instead we cite Elliott's example to highlight the fact that even riders who have had success using what may be described as 'traditional' training methods are prepared to move with the times. Just because a regime worked when you were in your twenties doesn't mean that you can't learn from modern advances in sports science. Indeed, as you get older it is more important to pay attention to how you train, because the effects of overtraining in the older athlete are potentially more damaging than they would be for a young rider.

2

PHYSIOLOGY AND TRAINING

5

BIKE BASICS

Before we look at training and nutrition, it's important to go through the basics, looking at the bikes you will use for training and racing and also how they are set up to give you the correct riding position. Getting these things right is essential before setting out on any training programme. If you are an experienced cyclist you may be familiar with these principles already, but even so it is still worth taking a look at this chapter because we aim to make you think about things that you may have taken for granted. So take some time to take a fresh look at the bikes and kit you use: you may be in for a surprise! We shall also take a look at riding skills and techniques that may help you make your training more efficient and safer.

How many times have you heard about a cyclist being helped up after a bad crash and asking

'How's my bike?' They may have broken bones, but it's always the machine they worry about first.

The point we are trying to make here is to keep things in perspective. The bike you ride is important, and in this chapter we will give you advice on what to look for in a training bike and on what type of machine you should use for sportive events. It would be no good turning up for the Étape du Tour on a Raleigh Chopper, but equally only professional riders can gain any real advantage from having a professional-level machine. We've all gone out and bought carbon fibre trick bits in the hope that they will make us that little bit faster. But saving a few grams on the bike is not always the way to find significant improvements in performance. Don't believe us? Then take a look at this.

Table 5.1 Typical biker's kit: weight loss, performance gain?

	Heavier option			Lighter option		
Component	Weight	Typical cost	Component	Weight	Typical cost
Saddle					
Selle Italia Flite Classic	180g	£82.49	Selle Italia SLR C64 Carbon	83g	£289.00
Seat post					
FSA SL-250 27.2/350mm	250g	£29.99	Campagnolo Record Carbon 27.2/350mm	185g	£120.99
Bottle cage					
Elite Ciussi Gel Steel	82g	£6.99	Tune Wassertrager	7g	£35.49
Quick Release					
Shimano Ultegra	121g	£24.00	Tune AC14	49g	£60.00
Stem					
ITM Forged Lux	137g	£29.99	Syntace F99 254 Stem 105mm with Ti	99g	£100.80
Total	770g	£173.46		423g	£606.28
Difference				347g	£432.82

For a cost of around £550 you could reduce the weight of your bike by around half a kilogram (1.1 lb). The performance gain from doing this would be minimal. As you will find in later chapters, improving fitness and reducing body fat gives significant improvements and at very little cost. So get a decent bike by all means, but don't ever be conned into thinking that going out and buying a bike twice as expensive is going to make you twice as good. It won't.

There's a story often told by Chris Boardman about his win in the Barcelona Olympics in 1992. There had been a lot of hype in the media about his Lotus 'super bike'. Some of the tabloid reports implied that his win had more to do with his revolutionary carbon fibre Lotus machine than with the athlete powering it around the track. Boardman says that he and his coach Peter Keen decided to find out just how good the bike was by standing it up against a wall at the side of the velodrome and watching it for 10 minutes to see how far it went.

The point is that you can go out and buy Boardman's bike, but it won't turn you into an Olympic champion or world record breaker. An obvious statement maybe, but it's worth reminding yourself of that fact the next time you find yourself drooling over a pair of carbon fibre pedals in your local bike shop on a Saturday afternoon when you should have been out training.

Which bike for training and which for racing?

The training bike

Most riders will have a bike for training and a bike for racing. It makes sense to protect your racing machine from the worst of the winter

Figure 5.1 The Kenesis Racelight T, a classic training bike.

weather. It will last longer and will be more reliable as a result. Getting a training bike that you can put mudguards on will make training in bad weather more comfortable. And if you're more comfortable you will get out and train more. The training bike should be of the same dimensions as your racing machine, with your position on the bike the same too. Cranks should be the same length, handlebars the same width and saddle the same height. Again, it may seem obvious, but there are many riders who have a different set-up on their training and racing bikes.

Choice of frame is really a personal one. Steel and titanium tend to be more comfortable than aluminium. Carbon fibre is the most popular frame material right now as it is comfortable, light and provides an efficient frame that is strongest where it needs to be: around the bottom bracket so there is no flex when sprinting or riding out of the saddle. However, you'll be hard-pushed to find a carbon fibre bike designed for winter training with full mudguards.

The most important thing is fit and reliability. Everything else is secondary. To make winter training more tolerable, it's worth investing in good quality winter tyres to reduce the risk of punctures. Nevertheless, remember to carry a pump (or CO_2 system) and spare tubes at all times.

The racing bike

As with the training bike, the main priority with your race bike is the fit. Frame materials are, again, a personal choice. Carbon fibre is now more affordable and provides a good balance between weight, strength and stiffness.

Figure 5.2 The Scott Addict LTD. At 790g, this bike is reported to be the lightest road frame in the world, and is a popular choice for many sportive and racing cyclists.

BIKE FRAME MATERIALS:
PROS AND CONS

CARBON FIBRE

Carbon fibre frames and forks are now the most popular choice for pro and amateur riders. The material offers a good balance of being lightweight, strong and comfortable. All bike frames are a compromise between these three factors. Up until a few years ago, carbon fibre was so expensive that it was only a choice for pro teams or club riders with money to burn. Now you can get a good quality carbon fibre machine for around £1,200. Carbon fibre has some inherent qualities which make it ideal for making bikes.

Because frames are most commonly made by weaving layers of carbon fibre together, they can be arranged so as to make the bike strongest where it needs to be. Carbon fibre frames are designed to be stiffer laterally than they are vertically. This means that the frame will absorb shock from the road, making it more comfortable to ride, but will not flex laterally, preventing any waste of energy caused by the bottom bracket flexing under maximum efforts such as sprinting or climbing out of the saddle. The downside to carbon fibre is that, if it is damaged, it is virtually impossible to repair. Also, carbon fibre can be damaged internally even though on the surface it looks perfect. This makes buying a second-hand carbon fibre machine a potential hazard; it is sometimes impossible to tell if a machine has been damaged in a crash.

ALUMINIUM

Aluminium frames became increasingly popular in the 1990s as they replaced traditional steel frames. It's light and stiff and gives a lively ride quality. The downside of aluminium frames is that they tend to be so rigid that they absorb little road vibration and can be uncomfortable on long rides. Aluminium will also fatigue over time so will not last a lifetime. Some manufacturers overcame this problem by building frames with aluminium main tubes and carbon fibre seat and chain stays. Combined with carbon fibre forks too, these frames had a good combination of comfort and performance.

STEEL

This is the original frame material dating back to the invention of the bicycle. In the post-war years, the vast majority of bikes for pros or amateurs in Europe were made of either Reynolds or Columbus tubing. There were innovations using different gauges of double-butted tubing, but essentially little radical development occurred until the 1980s, when more exotic materials like titanium, aluminium and carbon fibre began to challenge steel's dominance. The 1990s saw the end of steel as a choice for top-end road bikes and it was in this decade that steel's place in the Tour de France peloton came to an end. New grades of steel are now on the market and are proving popular because they can match some carbon, aluminium or titanium bikes in terms of weight.

Steel generally makes for a comfortable frame. It also has the advantage of being easier to work with, so finding someone who can build a frame customised to your specifications is less of a challenge. Steel is easier to repair than any other material used for bike frames. It is also one of the most durable materials, provided the frame is protected by anti-corrosion treatments.

TITANIUM

Titanium is considered by many to be the perfect material for frame-building. Top-quality titanium frames are light, durable and comfortable, as well as being incredibly strong. Because titanium does not corrode, it will last indefinitely. Many titanium frames are sold unpainted and simply polished.

The downside to titanium is that, even though there are a number of manufacturers who produce top-quality frames, they are all relatively expensive. Production costs are high because making titanium frames is a complicated business. Some titanium frames will also flex more than a carbon fibre or aluminium frame. Titanium frames are usually combined with carbon fibre forks. There are other technical reasons why titanium forks are impractical.

Choice of frame material

As you can see from the box above, there are many factors to consider when deciding which material to choose. The most important consideration in all of this is *always* that the bike you choose must be the right fit. There's no point buying a bike that is too big or too small.

Most people don't need a custom-made frame. Custom frames used to be something that all pro riders had, but now many pro riders get production frames that are customised to fit using different seat posts and handlebar stems. However, if you are very tall or very short then you may find that stock carbon fibre or aluminium frames may not be available in the size that you need. Because most carbon fibre frames are made with a mould costing hundreds of thousands of pounds to produce, most of us can't run to a custom-made carbon machine! But there are still many small manufacturers who produce custom-made steel frames at an affordable price.

If you are of average build then you have a choice of any frame material. The best thing is to try out a few machines, either from friends of a similar build or at bike shops that offer test rides. Ultimately it may come down to cost. You don't have to spend a fortune to get a race bike that will be adequate for riding sportives. But don't be tempted to buy £79.99 bikes advertised in the Sunday papers; they just won't be up to the job. If you go to a reputable bike shop, they should be able to get you a decent machine for around £800 upwards. Anything more than that is up to you.

In cycling, the more you spend the less you get – in terms of weight at least. Getting a super lightweight machine costing £5,000 will make virtually no difference to the performance of the average rider. If you have a bike that fits you properly, is comfortable and reliable and weighs in at around 8 kg (18 lb) give or take a few grams, you won't be at a serious disadvantage in sportive events. At the end of the day it's about the rider, not the bike. Now where have we heard that before!

Getting your gearing right

Because most sportives involve a good deal of climbing, it is important to consider gears and gear ratios.

Time was when all race bikes came with a standard 52x42 chainring set-up and a cassette with the biggest cog being a 23 or 24. If you're a Tour de France rider tackling a mountain stage, this set-up may be fine – although even most Tour riders would opt for a 39 ring instead of a 42. But for the average rider a more generous gear set-up is advisable. On long mountain climbs it is more efficient to spin smaller gears at a faster cadence than to grind out bigger gears at a slower pedalling rate. There are two options to consider. First, you can fit a triple chainset, which has three chainrings, typically 52x39x30 although you can customise most chainsets as you see fit. Combined with a 10-speed sprocket on the back wheel, this gives you a combination of 30 gear options. This will provide a wide range of gears and offers the option of a 'granny gear' for very steep climbs or for when you're suffering at the end of a long ride.

The other option is the so-called 'compact' chainset. These have become increasingly popular in recent years because they weigh a little less than triple chainsets and can be easily fitted to a bike that has a double chainset set-up.

The compact chainset is one whose crank arm has a smaller 'spider' – that is, the section where the chainrings are bolted on to the cranks has a smaller diameter, allowing smaller rings to be attached.

A typical compact chainset will have a 50x36 or a 48x34 chainring set-up. This gives a better range of gears than a standard double chainset, but not as wide a range as a triple. Some people prefer triples; others prefer compacts. There's no definite answer as to which is best, but here are some points to consider when making your choice.

Most compact chainsets will work with a standard double STI (Shimano) or Ergo (Campag) brake/gear lever. Changing from a double set-up to a triple will often require a new brake/gear lever and a new front and rear mechanism.

Triples offer a greater range of gear ratios; compacts mean you will often end up with a smaller top gear to accommodate having a smaller bottom gear. So with a triple you can have a 52x11 top gear, whereas with a compact you might only have a 50x11. This will only make a real difference on very fast descents and even then may not be that noticeable in terms of speed achieved.

Fitting a compact means having greater jumps between gears, due to the difference in the size of the chainrings. So you may find that riding with a compact means sometimes not being able to find just the right gear in certain terrain. You may find one gear is too high and the next one down too low. With a triple you will usually be able to find the perfect combination to maintain the correct cadence.

And finally, there are still some riders who believe that riding a double is a sign of a 'real' racing cyclist and riding a triple is the sign of a tourist. Well, there are many riders who head into the Alps on a double and end up pedalling at 30 rpm, only to be overtaken by someone spinning a triple at 90 rpm. At the end of the day it's about getting from A to B as fast as you can. If a triple suits your riding style or the terrain better than a double then that's all that matters.

Even pro riders use triples sometimes. In the Tour of Spain there is a climb called the Angrilu, which is widely regarded as one of the toughest road climbs used in any race anywhere in the world. It has sections as steep as one in three (33 per cent) and top riders often use triples on that stage. Roberto Heras, who rode for Lance Armstrong's US Postal Service team, won on the Angrilu on a Trek bike fitted with a Shimano triple chainset.

Bike set-up and riding position

As we have discussed already, the most important factor about your bike is that it fits you properly. There's no point in having a state-of-the-art machine if it is too big or too small for you. Before deciding on the right frame size for you, it is important to get a few measurements.

Remember that with most modern bikes, and especially those that have a 'compact' frame design, it is possible to produce a wide range of riding positions by adjusting the lengths of the seat pin and handlebar stem. But the starting point must always be the saddle height and fore and aft position. Never alter your riding position by changing the handlebar stem length or handlebar height to fit in with the saddle position.

The right frame size

Getting the right saddle height position is connected to getting the right frame size. You want a frame size that allows for a good portion of the seat pin to extend out of the frame, but not so far that it goes beyond the limit marked on the seat pin. Find your correct saddle height, and then make sure you can achieve this position on your current bike. If you can't, take your saddle height measurement to your local bike shop and use it to choose a new frame of the correct size.

Finding your correct saddle height

Start by placing your current bike on a turbo trainer and wear your normal cycling shoes. Pedal for five minutes or so to get you warmed up, thus making sure that your muscles are relaxed. This also allows you to settle into your normal riding position.

Unclip your feet from the pedals; put both your heels on the pedals and pedal slowly. You should be able to pedal in this way with your legs fully extended at the bottom of each pedal stroke. But your heels should not lose contact with the pedals; if they do, your saddle is too high. You should also be able to pedal without your hips rocking from side to side; again, if this happens you need to lower the saddle slightly and try the test again. Conversely, if your legs are not fully extended while pedalling with your heels then the saddle is too low.

If, by applying these methods, you find that your current saddle position is way out, it is advisable to alter the position gradually over a few weeks rather than adjusting it straight away and going on a training ride. For example, if your current saddle height is a lot lower than it should be, raise the saddle by 5 mm and ride it like that for a week. The next week raise it by another 5 mm

and ride for a week. Continue this process until the correct saddle height is reached.

The reason for doing this is that raising the saddle by several centimetres in one go may place strain on muscles and ligaments not used to riding in a more stretched-out position. By adjusting the seat position gradually, you lessen the risk of injury. Just as your body adapts slowly to training stimulus, it also takes time to become accustomed to a different riding position. It's worth taking time to get your saddle height right. If it's too high, you will be stretching too much, which may lead to muscle strains. It will also make it difficult for you to 'spin' gears quickly, making you less efficient on the bike. A saddle that is too low will mean that you are not able to exert the maximum amount of power through the pedals.

Saddle fore and aft position

Now that you have your saddle height adjusted correctly, you can adjust the fore and aft position. Again, it is important to get this right because your fore and aft position affects where your feet are in relation to the pedals, which in turn influences your pedalling efficiency.

The ideal is to have the front part of your knee directly over the pedal axle when the cranks are horizontal. Before you get back on the bike, you will need a plumb line: you can make one by tying a small weight to a piece of string. To start, you should sit on the bike in a comfortable position, with your backside in the centre of the saddle.

Once you have warmed up for a few minutes, turn the pedals until the cranks are horizontal. Take the plumb line and position the end of the piece of string so that it is touching the front part of your knee. The string should fall through the pedal spindle; if it doesn't, you need to adjust the saddle forwards or backwards to get the right position.

Handlebar height and reach
Aerodynamics is important in making bike and rider as efficient as possible. But there is always a compromise to be made between aerodynamics and comfort. A lot of pro riders will have their handlebars set very low and will be able to adopt an extremely aerodynamic position. Some club riders see this and are tempted to try to use an equally low position. Some can do it, but most will find it uncomfortable and as a result will not tend to ride with their hands on drops. It is better to set up the bars slightly higher, so that the rider is encouraged to use the drops more and so improve their aerodynamic position. It is really a question of how supple the rider is. Some riders can adopt really low positions and be comfortable, while others can't.

The distance you have to reach to the handlebars is also important and may require trying different length handlebar stems to get it right. Once you have your saddle height and fore and aft position adjusted, place your left elbow against the tip of the saddle and hold out your forearm horizontally with your fingers

outstretched. Now place your right hand at 90 degrees to your left hand, with the edge of your right hand touching the tip of the middle finger of your left hand. The little finger on your right hand should be in line with the centre of the handlebars. You will need a new stem if this is not the case. This method is an approximation and you may wish to experiment with different stem lengths. The key is always to adopt a position in which you are neither too stretched nor too cramped, with your weight distributed equally between the saddle and the handlebars.

Handlebar width is easy to determine: just choose a set of handlebars that are the same width as your shoulders.

Specialist advice
Many companies now offer the use of 'bike fit' systems to get the correct frame size and riding position. Lots of these systems are set up in bike shops and are fine if you go somewhere reputable. But for most people they are not essential, provided you're confident that you know enough about the position you need. If you have legs of unequal length, or are extremely tall or short, then getting checked out with the aid of a bike fit system may be advisable.

6

RIDING SKILLS AND TECHNIQUES

'Throughout the race you are thinking about conserving energy. You want to have as big a sugar cube as you can at the end of the race.'
Pro rider Mark Cavendish

Riding efficiently

How efficient are you on the bike? We all like to think that we pedal with the grace and economy of effort of seven-times Tour de France winner Lance Armstrong or, for those of you with longer memories, Stephen Roche. In 1987 Roche won the Tour de France, Giro d'Italia and World Championship road races. The only other rider to achieve that triple crown in one season was Eddy Merckx.

We may all like to believe that we have the smooth riding style of Armstrong or Roche, but the truth is often less flattering. We can all benefit from improving skills such as following a wheel in order to maximise the amount of energy we save by slipstreaming other riders. Paying attention to your riding style and technique is important if you want to perform to your potential in competition.

As Mark Cavendish reminds us in his quote above, it's all about 'the sugar cube': the amount of energy you have available to turn into muscle power. Much of this book is devoted to optimising your aerobic fitness and making sure your diet and nutrition strategies during a race give you the maximum amount of energy. But if you then waste a lot of that energy due to poor pedalling technique or poor riding skills much of that dedication in training will be wasted too.

La souplesse

Literally *la souplesse* means suppleness. It's how the French describe a good pedalling technique: the fluid, apparently effortless style displayed by riders like Armstrong and by top-class track riders turned roadmen like Cavendish and Bradley Wiggins.

It is a skill that comes naturally to some, but that can be learned by all of us to varying degrees if we put in the time and effort. If you have time to ride a fixed-wheel bike, the track is a good place to start. The fixed wheel means the rider has to turn the pedals as long as the wheels are going round. This forces the rider to concentrate on pedalling smoothly at high cadence. You can, of course, adapt a road bike to run with a fixed wheel, but be careful if you are new to riding a fixed as it takes a bit of getting used to.

Riding some sessions on a track with a fixed-gear track bike will also help improve your pedalling technique. Concentrate on pedalling smoothly, pushing down with one foot as you pull up with the other. At the bottom of each pedal stroke, imagine that you are trying to wipe your feet on a doormat and you will get the idea of pulling up on the pedal stroke. This technique utilises the calf muscles and improves the power you are able to generate on each stroke. Alternatively, you can develop your pedalling technique as a warm-up during turbo training sessions.

Riding in a group

In an event like the Étape du Tour you can find yourself in the middle of 250 to 300 riders. So, if you have spent most of your time on the bike riding alone, you must get used to riding in a group. Joining in with your local club ride, or entering smaller sportive or audax events, is a good place to start.

Group riding has its own rules and etiquette. Riders at the front of the group act as guides for everyone behind. They will often signal to everyone if there are potholes ahead or if the group is going to have to slow down at a junction. Getting used to the changes in pace, and having to think about cyclists in front of you, behind you and at your side, is an important skill to learn.

Also, being able to ride on someone's wheel is essential if you are to ride as efficiently as possible. Sitting behind one rider at 40 km/h (25 mph), the amount of oxygen you need is reduced by approximately 23 per cent. Riding at the back of a group of four riders, the reduction in oxygen cost is 30 per cent. Sitting behind a vehicle, which is equivalent to riding behind a large group of riders, gives an oxygen-cost saving of 63 per cent (the full impact of this will become evident later in the book). Riding team time trials, or just practising riding in a small group with your club mates, is often enough to develop this skill if you do it sufficiently frequently. This is particularly important if you are coming to sportive riding from a purely time-trialling background or after training alone. Developing your ability to follow a wheel will allow you to reduce your oxygen cost in a race and thus save energy.

Climbing

A common misconception is that, if you are riding up a short, steep climb, it is okay to power up it by getting out of the saddle and using your body weight to get you over the top. In fact, this can rapidly eat into limited energy stores and cause you to suffer fatigue much earlier in the ride than you would have done otherwise. Going into oxygen debt may be worthwhile, however, if it means staying in contact with a fast-moving group, which can result in significant energy savings.

On longer climbs, such as those you will face in the Alps and Pyrenees, you should aim to stay seated and spin small gears. That doesn't mean continuously spinning at 120 rpm like Armstrong attacking the final decisive climb of a stage. What we mean is spinning at a steady cadence of between 85 and 95 rpm in a gear that feels relatively easy. The key is to be able to sustain your cadence and level of effort for the duration of the climb by adjusting your gears to suit the gradient. This is the most efficient way of tackling long climbs and you should practise it as often as possible. It also helps if you have done your homework about the climbs you will face.

There are many websites that offer useful information about some of the more well-known climbs, especially European climbs used regularly in major stage races like the Tour de France and Giro d'Italia. Knowing the length of climbs and the gradient is a big help in judging the level of effort you feel you can sustain over the whole climb.

TIPS FROM THE TOP
pro rider Mark Cavendish on climbing

Cavendish is a sprinter, but he has shown he can get over some big climbs and win – as he did when he took hilly stage wins in the Tour of Catalunya in Spain in 2007. He is tipped as a future winner of the green points jersey in the Tour de France, so he will hope to improve his climbing ability in years to come. As a rider who aims to survive mountain stages in the Tour de France, rather than be at the front with the mountain specialists, he is a good man to ask about pacing yourself on long climbs. He tends not to pay too much attention to his pulse monitor during a race, but believes they are useful in pacing yourself on a long climb.

Knowing roughly what heart rate you can sustain over a long climb is something you need to consider before the race. It is worth keeping a record of any training efforts on long climbs to get an idea of what heart rate you can ride to in a race.

Cornering

In Figure 6.1, notice how Peter Kennaugh's upper body is bent over the bike to lower his centre of gravity and make the bike more stable. Notice also how he is just touching the rear brake to reduce his speed going into the corner. His right leg is pushing his body weight down on the right pedal, which increases the traction of the tyres and gives maximum grip through the corner.

Cornering involves braking and accelerating; being able to ride through corners as fast as possible will save you a lot of energy. You may already feel that you are good at cornering but, if you often find yourself going through corners and losing contact with the rider in front, you may need to work on your technique. The key to developing good cornering skills is to go back to basics and work on the elements involved – assessing the corner, taking the right line and braking correctly.

Assessing the corner involves several considerations. Is the rider in front braking hard? Can you see through the corner? Is the surface rough or is the road wet? All of this may seem like second nature, but if you have trouble cornering fast, these are the issues you must reconsider if you are to improve.

It's worth practising on quiet, familiar roads, or you could even use cones to mark out a corner in a car park. Practise it again and again to get your line right, while gradually building up your speed. Good technique comes before speed. There's no sense in just throwing yourself into corners at breakneck pace if your technique is all wrong. Work on developing your skills and your speed will naturally improve.

As you approach fast corners, it is best to have your hands on the drops: this lowers your centre

Figure 6.1 The correct line to take in corners. The picture on the bottom right shows Great Britain Olympic Academy rider Peter Kennaugh

of gravity and gives you more control over the bike. Visualise trying to steer the bike by slightly shifting your sitting position. Remember, bikes counter-steer when riding at speed; for example, if you try to turn the handlebars to the left, the bike will go right. Of course, handling is different when riding at low speed. We don't need to go

into the physics here, but if you are new to cycling or struggle with cornering it's worth experimenting with counter-steering.

With your hands positioned correctly, and your balance and centre of gravity adjusted, you are set up correctly. As you corner, you must also try to keep your head level. As you will see from Figure 6.1, the correct line is aimed at 'straightening' the corner as much as possible. That is to say, you must aim to take the smoothest and fastest line. Go wide as you approach and brake before you start to turn. Safety, of course, must be your priority. If you are racing on closed roads, you can use all of the road. On open roads you must stay in your lane. The risks involved far outweigh any possible gain.

Your aim is to take the line that cuts across the apex of the corner. Finding a friend who has good bike-handling skills, and is faster than you in corners, can be a good way to improve. Choose a circuit on a quiet road and get them to ride with you following their wheel. Ask them to take it easy to begin with and aim to follow their line and pay attention to when they brake. As you get more confident, you can ask them to speed up and gradually improve your own cornering ability.

Descending

The skills and techniques required to descend well are essentially the same as those required for cornering. The only difference is that the speed involved is higher, so the time you have to assess and prepare for a bend or corner will be significantly reduced. We've all seen riders in the Tour de France who climb mountains like they have wings, but then seem to lose their ability to fly on the descent. Of course, a good climber will gain more time on a long ascent in the Alps than they will ever lose on the descent. But practising your descending skills is worth doing not only to

save time, but also to stay safe. On fast descents it is important to always be in control of your bike. Any potholes or debris in the road will not be as easy to avoid at higher speeds.

There's also an advantage to be gained by making yourself as aerodynamic as possible in order to reduce drag. You may have seen Tour de France riders adopting extreme aerodynamic positions on the bike to gain a few more seconds on a descent. Riders may slide their backside off the front of the saddle and sit on the top tube of the bike.

Tour de France and Giro d'Italia winner Marco Pantani used to slide off the back of his saddle and rest his belly on it to get a more tucked position – sometimes he even tucked one arm behind his back! It is debatable whether either of these extreme positions offer any advantage in terms of speed. What is beyond question is that they both pose a risk to the rider and those around them because they reduce the amount of control the rider has over their bike.

If you are going so fast that your highest gear has 'spun out' – that is to say, you can't pedal fast enough to produce any more speed from the bike – then an aero tuck is advisable. But stick to more conventional tuck positions. Put your hands on the drops of the handlebars so you can easily manoeuvre the bike and be within reach of the brakes. Position the pedals so that the crank arms are parallel to the ground. Bring your knees in to touch the top tube and tuck your head down low.

This tuck position was good enough for generations of riders until some top pros decided to experiment with more extreme positions in recent years. Getting down the descent safely is the main aim. A crash at 80 km/h (50 mph) is going to cost you a lot more time than a few fractions of a second saved by hanging your backside off the back of the bike.

TIPS FROM THE TOP
*Great Britain Olympic Academy rider
Jonny Bellis on descending*

If you are not the best when it comes to descending, Bellis has a few tips on improving your technique. Usually a rider would position their hands on the drop handlebars of a road bike because this gives the best control for descending. A drill used by the Great Britain team to improve descending skills is to get riders to put their hands on the tops of the handlebars because this makes the bike more difficult to control. Riding descents like this can help you improve your handling of the bike, and you'll notice the benefit when you go back to using the drops in a race.

Bellis says the most important thing about cornering and descending is braking correctly, adjusting your speed before you go into a corner so that you, at most, only have to touch the back brake if you are going slightly too fast.

Practice makes perfect

Like any other skill, the more time you spend practising these techniques, the better you will become. But this doesn't mean that you have to carry out specific drills to improve the skills discussed in this chapter. Group riding, climbing, cornering and descending can all be practised as part of regular training rides. The main point of this chapter is to get you to think about these skills and identify any areas where you are weak. Use the time you have to train not just to develop your fitness, but also to concentrate on the core skills that will maximise your performance.

It may not seem likely that such improvements will make a lot of difference, but remember there are big advantages to gain from small changes. Sportive rides are often 160 km (100 miles) or more: that's a lot of corners, descents and climbs. If you can gain just a small percentage of speed in corners, that can add up to a big gain on a long ride. Tactics also play a part. If you are in a fast-moving group but get dropped due to not being able to corner or descend fast enough, you face a long haul on your own and you've missed a chance to get an easier and faster ride to the finish. Improving your riding skills will pay dividends on race day.

TIPS FROM THE TOP

pro rider Mark Cavendish on riding skills

'Don't bottle it,' is Mark Cavendish's advice when asked how to improve cornering skills or any other aspect of bike handling. He says the most common error is for riders to panic when things start to go wrong. They then make the wrong decision or hesitate too long before reacting to correct a mistake. Say you're going into a corner and you hit a patch of diesel or gravel. Some riders will panic and hit the brakes: the worst thing you can do.

'Hesitation is the mother of all screw-ups,' says Cavendish, who won 11 road races in his first season as a pro. 'It's like when you are in a car and it starts to skid and someone panics and puts their foot on the brake and makes it worse. It's the same on a bike: people panic and hit the brakes.'

Cavendish says that major tyre firms have spent a lot of money in research to make modern bike tyres incredibly 'grippy' in corners. He says investing in a good set of quality tyres can improve both safety and cornering speeds.

Knowing that you have a good set of tyres also improves a rider's confidence when cornering. If Cavendish is in a bunch on a descent, as he was when he made his debut in the Tour de France in 2007, he will often ride with his hands on top of the bars instead of the drops. This allows him to get a better view of the road ahead as he sits higher up and can see beyond the riders in front.

7

THE SCIENCE OF CYCLING

The physiological demands of sportive riding

All sportives are different and each has different challenges to overcome. You should bear this in mind when training for the event you have chosen. There's not much sense in doing loads of hill training if you are preparing for a sportive that doesn't have any hills in it. But there are some factors that are common to all or most sportives. And the most important is the fact that they are all endurance events, even though distances may vary from 60 km (37 miles) up to 260 km (162 miles). As such, the key to all sportive riding is improving endurance.

Most sportives, however, will include some hills or even mountains to climb. In events like the Étape du Tour, there will be several high mountain passes to conquer, meaning that improving your climbing ability will be a key factor in improving your performance.

Figure 7.1 shows the power profile of a professional rider in the 2007 Tour de France, on the same stage as was used for the Étape. It clearly shows the high power required for the climbs, with the athlete maintaining nearly 500 watts for sustained periods, and also the constant workload throughout the rest of the stage. Similarly, several scientific studies have shown that in the high mountain stages of major tours, the professional riders will often maintain around 250 watts for the duration of a six-hour stage. Clearly, these are not easy rides in the French countryside.

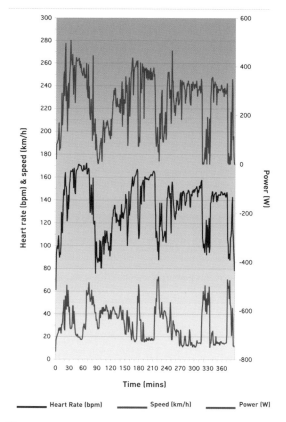

Figure 7.1 Power profile of a professional rider during stage 15 of the 2007 Tour de France, which was used for the Étape du Tour. Data courtesy of SRM.de

Choosing your event

You may choose a particular event for many reasons. It could be that you want to ride in a particular country or have agreed to ride with a friend in a particular race. But if your aim is to be as competitive as possible, you may want to read on.

There will be events that suit your natural talents more than others. A Tour de France rider is a fundamentally different athlete from a track sprinter. Their natural physiology will be different, as will their training.

The 2004 Olympic kilometre time-trial champion Chris Hoy is one of the fastest track riders in the world, but his natural talents and training suit him to short efforts of all-out speed. Hoy has ridden the Étape du Tour, and in a good time, but he could never hope to be competitive in that race because he is not built for endurance. Likewise, seven-time Tour de France winner Lance Armstrong wouldn't stand a chance in a kilometre time-trial against Hoy.

The point we are making here is that you need to think about the type of athlete you are. You can train to develop your sprinting speed or endurance and anyone can make improvements if they train properly. But we all have natural abilities that give us a predisposition towards events involving endurance, speed or power. In cycling, your body type will give you more of an advantage in some events than others. Chris Hoy, for example, while lean and muscular, is far heavier than most Tour de France riders. His muscular physique gives him power, which is great if you want to ride fast in track sprints. But in a race like the Tour de France, that physique would be a distinct disadvantage. In the Tour, riders have to be able to climb big mountain passes and power alone isn't sufficient.

Being a good climber is about having a high power-to-weight ratio; that is, producing a lot of power per kilogram of body weight. This tends to favour smaller, lighter riders, which is why the organisers of the Tour de France don't need to make the King of the Mountains jersey in any sizes except small and medium. Most sportive rides are very hilly and, if you are small and light, you should be able to ride well given the right training. If your physique is suited to being a good climber you should go for the most mountainous events you can find, like the Étape du Tour or Gran Fondo Campagnolo. The long continental climbs they feature will allow you to gain the most advantage from your abilities.

However, if you are well over 1.8 m (6 feet) tall and weigh in at around 95 kg (210 lb) such hilly races are not going to suit you. We are not saying that someone of such a physique cannot ride the Étape. It's achievable given the right training and especially if you are muscular and lean rather than overweight. But if you are a tall, heavy rider and you want to be as competitive as possible it is better to find events that don't have so many long climbs. Races like the Tour of Flanders or Amstel Gold sportives may be better suited to you because they feature shorter, steeper climbs that favour powerful riders.

Choosing an event that's ideal for your abilities may be a question of looking at your skill level as a cyclist as well as your fitness level. Sportives like the Tour of Flanders that feature cobbled climbs require better bike-handling skills than an Étape du Tour, so this is something that you may want to think about too.

The physiology of training

'Ride the bike. Ride the bike. Ride the bike.' Eddie Merckx to a young rider who had asked him how to become a better cyclist

So, you want to go faster?

Eddy Merckx is regarded by most experts as the greatest cyclist of all time. And with a palmarès (or record of race wins) that includes five Tour de France triumphs, victories in every major stage race and classic, and the world hour record, we are not about to disagree with that assessment.

What we do disagree with is his advice on training. Merckx was certainly an innovator and there was more to his training regime than just a massive amount of mileage. But his comment sums up the traditional attitude towards training: the belief that only a high-volume regime would produce any significant results.For years many club riders believed that if this approach worked for their cycling heroes, then it must work for them too. Go out and pile up the miles. And if your results aren't what you expected it must be because you are not riding enough. So go out and do some more!

With advances in sports science, we now know of course that such high-volume training will produce improvement in those physically capable of enduring such training loads. But for ordinary club riders, it is often a recipe for disaster. For club riders having to train after a hard day's work, it was also folly to expect that they could recover from each training session.

Elite riders, of course, have more time to rest after each day's training. If you can't race like a Tour de France champion, it's not realistic to expect to be able to train like one.

The philosophy of this book is that more is not necessarily better; in fact, it is often *worse*. Merckx was a phenomenal rider, especially when you consider the sheer volume of racing and training that he had to endure because of pressure from sponsors to compete week after week. How much better would he have been had he had the benefit of modern training methods? How many Tours de France would he have won if he'd had the luxury of focusing on that one race in the same way that Lance Armstrong did? Four-times world pro pursuit champion Hugh Porter, who raced against Merckx on the road and on the track, is now the BBC's cycling commentator. He reckons Merckx would have won 10 Tours if he had been able to prepare for the race in the way that Armstrong did.

There's no point in a coach telling a cyclist to go out and train for 15 hours a week if they are already exhausted trying to fit eight hours of training into a busy lifestyle. In this chapter we will outline the philosophy of our approach to training tailored to suit the needs of the individual. The old adage 'no pain, no gain' does not apply any more. Yes, some of the training sessions we will suggest will be hard and it will require focus and motivation to complete the schedule we will help you construct. But we believe that the results will speak for themselves. The adage now is simply to 'train smart'.

The building blocks of training

Before deciding on what training you need, it is essential to look first at the demands of the event you are facing. Every sportive ride is different, but there are some common elements to each. They are all long-distance, endurance events. They will, for the most part, involve a good deal of climbing. It is up to you to sit down and look at the event you have chosen to do and consider the demands involved. This is a process of goal-setting.

The athlete should set themselves short-, medium- and long-term goals. For an elite athlete, the long-term competitive goal may be winning the Olympic final in four years' time, with a medium-term goal of participating in a world championship. For you, the long-term goal will be a big sportive ride maybe six or eight months away. Medium-term goals, such as other sportives prior to your main goal, can be used as training and as a way of assessing your progress.

Goal-setting

Many people find goal-setting difficult. It shouldn't be that way. Goals are best if they are clear and have measurable outcomes. These will not always be easy to achieve, but should give a stepping stone to the priority event, or long-term goals. Goals can be both of a training nature and targetted towards competitive events.

In training, longer-term goals may often be something like aiming to improve your performance time, overall placing, or even just finishing a specific event. Medium-term goals may be trying to achieve a certain distance in a training ride, or achieving a certain amount of weight loss. Short-term goals will often focus on completing a certain amount of training within the next week, or even achieving heart rate targets for the training session that is just about to be undertaken. Once you have set your long-term goal, you can work backwards to decide how best to prepare to meet the challenge you have set yourself.

Training has to be sports specific. That is, you must prepare your body to cope with the demands made of it on race day. If your chosen sportive is a flat 100 km (62 miles) ride, there is little point doing extensive hill-training sessions or rides of 200 km (124 miles) or more. It may sound obvious, but it's a mistake many people make. There are lots of time-triallists around who never compete in events longer than 16 km (10 miles), but who go out and do training rides of between four and six hours for an event that will take them less than half an hour.

So take some time to think about the ride you have entered. How far is it; how much climbing will there be; how steep will the climbs be? What are the weather conditions likely to be? And what about the skills needed to complete the ride? Are you used to riding in large groups of riders? Are your cornering and descending skills sufficient to enable you to stay with a fast-moving group on a technically demanding mountain descent? All these factors should be considered before preparing your training programme.

Another factor to think about is getting your priorities right. Many riders believe that getting the same bike that Lance Armstrong rode to victory in the Tour de France will give them an advantage in a sportive ride. But if you are a rider who is carrying around a few spare kilograms of body fat, there is little point in spending thousands on a bike that will only save you a kilogram at most.

In our work at Sportstest, we often see experienced riders who train for many hours a week while carrying anything up to 8 kg (17.6 lb) of body fat that they could easily lose with a bit more thought to training and diet. Concentrating on the bike rather than their own fitness is a classic case of looking for a short cut to improved performance. The truth is that there are no short cuts.

But you don't necessarily have to train harder to get significant performance gains through training and better nutrition. You just need to train with a more scientific approach and this will give you much more in the way of improved performance than any bike you could buy.

Of all endurance athletes, cyclists are probably the most guilty when it comes to looking for short cuts to improved performance by buying new equipment. We want you to get away from that thought process and concentrate on improving your abilities as an athlete. The bike is a tool that allows you to do a job. But you supply the power, you are the engine and you have the ability to fine-tune that engine to cope with the demands of a sportive ride.

Determinants of performance

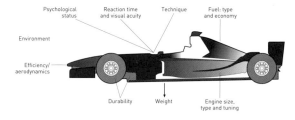

Psychological status

Reaction time and visual acuity

Technique

Fuel: type and economy

Environment

Efficiency/ aerodynamics

Durability

Weight

Engine size, type and tuning

Figure 7.2 The analogy with a Formula One car

The analogy of a Formula One car (Figure 7.2) may seem a little out of place when talking about improving your performance as a cyclist. But it is a great way of explaining how you must think about the factors that affect how fast and how far you can ride. The key difference, of course, between the car and the cyclist is that the rider provides the power.

As we have already discussed, the training you require will be different depending on the event you are aiming to do well in. It's the same with the Formula One car. It is perfect for a race lasting around two hours on a track. It wouldn't be much use in an off-road rally or a 24-hour endurance event like Le Mans. The Formula One car is built specifically for the demands of a Grand Prix. In the same way, we aim to prepare you specifically for the demands of a sportive ride.

In other chapters we will look at factors such as aerodynamics, pedalling efficiency and nutrition, that can be improved to make the most of the power that your 'engine' produces. But first we will look at the engine itself: how you as a rider can train yourself to produce more power for a longer period. The bigger a car's engine, the more power it can produce and the faster it will go. But let's say we build a car that has a dual-fuel system comprising a petrol engine and an electric engine. This is more akin to the body's own energy systems. At low speeds, the electric system is adequate to provide the power we need. This is comparable to the body's fat-burning energy system.

As speed increases, the car will use petrol to provide sufficient power, and the human body will start to burn carbohydrate. If the car then needs to accelerate even faster, it may use a fuel injection system that will cause a rapid increase in the rate at which petrol is burned. The body uses fast-twitch muscle fibres to provide such power in a sprint and this will rapidly burn carbohydrate. These fast-twitch fibres are called type 2b, and they are essentially anaerobic fibres: that is, they function without the use of oxygen. To adapt your 'engine' to the demands of sportive riding, you will have to train. Let's take a look at the factors that determine the effectiveness of training.

The five keys elements of training

An effective training programme has to include five different components.

1 Adequate volume

This is specific to the individual and dependent on how much time you can realistically devote to training. If you are a full-time professional, adequate volume may mean more than 20–30 hours per week. This is obviously a huge demand for a club-level rider with work and family commitments. That said, if you feel able to devote 10 hours per week to training it does not necessarily follow that this is the training volume you should aim for. If training 10 hours per week leaves you overtrained and exhausted after a month, it serves no purpose to carry on with such a workload. There will, of course, be other riders who only respond to higher volumes of training and are able to cope with this extra workload.

2 Appropriate duration

This means a training ride duration appropriate to the intensity you are maintaining. For example, 'endurance zone' rides should be around 90 minutes to two hours long, because this is the optimal duration for such a training intensity. Riding at this intensity for longer won't produce greater physiological benefits. It's what many coaches refer to as the mile of diminishing returns. There is a point in any training session where continuing won't bring any more gains and will simply cause greater fatigue and delay the recovery process before your next training session.

3 Sufficient intensity

Everyone has been on club rides where there are first category riders cruising along at the front happily chatting away to each other, while third and fourth category riders are hanging out the back desperately trying to hold on to the bunch. Training in groups like this for four or five hours usually means that the ride is too easy for the first cats and too hard for the thirds and fourths.

What we mean by sufficient intensity is that any training ride has to be performed at a level appropriate to the duration and to the purpose of the session. There's little point doing a 20-minute rider at a very low intensity unless it is as a recovery ride. Equally, going out on the club chain gang and doing five hours at race pace with riders far stronger than you is not the optimal way to improve fitness.

During his time with the South African Institute of Sport, co-author Garry Palmer worked with one elite rider who was doing eight-hour training rides in hilly terrain, but his heart rate was only maintaining an effective training heart rate for about an hour. So he was spending seven hours of wasted time on his bike. That's nice if you just want to enjoy the sunshine, but not so good if you want to get the maximum benefit out of the time you have available to train.

4 Sports specificity

Training on your bike is the best way to improve performance as a cyclist. There are many riders who will use other activities to stay in shape in the winter months, whether it's doing gym circuits or weight training. There may be some occasions when such work is necessary, particularly if an individual has a muscle imbalance or is recovering from injury. But the bulk of the training you do must be specific to the sport in which you wish to compete. Likewise, it makes sense for a mountain biker who cannot always train off-road to use their mountain bike on the road, or train on a road bike with the same riding position and gearing as they use on their mountain bike. Time-triallists should do as much training as they can on their time-trial machine to make their preparation as specific as possible to their chosen discipline.

5 Optimal recovery

Training prompts physiological changes in the body, but it is during recovery that the developments that make an individual better adapted to cope with the physical demands of racing occur. Without adequate recovery, these changes will not be completed before the next training session. Lack of adequate recovery time will also lead to overtraining and fatigue, which will prevent effective training development. Knowing when to rest, and how long to rest for, is a vital key to developing an effective training programme.

The overload principle

After a hard training session, the body will be fatigued and will have incurred some loss of carbohydrate energy stores. It may even have suffered some minor muscle damage. If, for example, an average rider had cycled 40 km (25 miles) in 75 minutes and felt fatigued afterwards, they may not be able to recover sufficiently to cycle the same route under

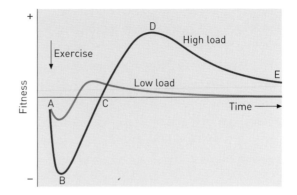

Figure 7.3 The overload principle

the same conditions in the same time 24 hours later.

Consider Figure 7.3. Supposing an athlete starts a training session with 'fitness' at point A. Training suppresses the level of performance of which the body is capable. As the session progresses, fatigue results, and the 'fitness' or ability to perform is depressed to point B, where the training session ends. But give the body time to recover, and fitness will return to point C. Ultimately, given appropriate recovery and adequate nutrition, it overcompensates by repairing muscle tissue and replacing carbohydrate stores to allow it to cope with this increased physical demand to point D. Should no further training take place, this increase in fitness will drop back to baseline (point E), or even below.

If this process is repeated over weeks and months, and if each session is started at the peak of recovery (point D), the body will show significant improvements in terms of the physical demand it is capable of coping with. This is how fitness improves through training. The key is to allow the body sufficient time to recover between training sessions so that the athlete avoids the damaging effects of overtraining. If you continue to train before recovery is complete (somewhere between points B and C), you get a gradual decline in performance as opposed to a steady increase. This will soon lead to overtraining.

Periodisation

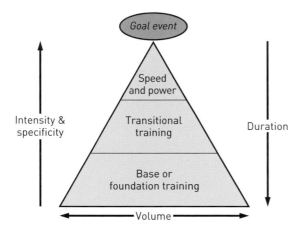

Figure 7.4 The training pyramid

Most cyclists will be familiar with the idea of a training programme being described as a pyramid. Figure 7.4 shows how the base of the pyramid involves the lowest intensity training and the highest volume. As you work your way up the pyramid, the volume decreases as the intensity increases. We will employ a system of periodisation – that is to say, training will be split up into blocks building up to race day.

Before we start to determine how your training will be structured, you must first decide how much time you have available to train. There is little point in us saying that you should do 20 hours a week if the demands of work and family life mean that you never have more than 10 hours available. Don't be worried if you can only manage to train five or six hours a week. You will be amazed at how much improvement can be made on such a programme. Chris Boardman won the Olympic pursuit title at the 1992 Barcelona games, allegedly on the back of between eight and ten hours a week of training. Tour de France riders will clock up massive amounts of miles in training, but you must remember that these are exceptionally gifted athletes and full-time professionals. If you can't race like Lance Armstrong, why should you expect to train like him?

Start by writing down your time commitments each week, including work, home life and leisure time. Be honest with yourself and work out exactly how much time you have free to train each week. This is the starting point in building our schedule.

You also need to assess your strengths and weaknesses. If you are a strong rider on the flat but always struggle on climbs, then this is an area you need to focus on. There may be other factors related to riding skills, such as being comfortable riding in a bunch or descending at speed. All such factors can affect your performance and need to be identified if they are weak areas. It's worth asking a coach or club mates to give you feedback on your own strengths and weaknesses: they may spot things that you are not aware of.

From here we can begin to plan the training phases. Broadly speaking, the training programme will be structured as in Figure 7.4. It begins with a broad base of high-volume, low-intensity work, progressing to a transitional phase that introduces shorter, higher intensity efforts. As race day approaches, volume decreases again while intensity is maintained. This is the broad picture, but within that we will have training cycles that involve weeks that build volume, followed by a week of recovery to allow the body to overcompensate for the effects of training and progress to a higher fitness level.

In the broad view illustrated by Figure 7.4, a sportive rider may focus as much as nine months, or as little as three months, on improving their base fitness. The transitional training will then be a block of somewhere between 6 and 12 weeks (dependent on the rider's needs and ambitions), and will focus mostly on higher intensity threshold work to develop climbing and race pace ability. The final phase of speed and power is used for sharpening towards a key event. For the sportive rider, this may be overlooked with minimal consequences. However, if your ambitions are to perform at your peak, and possibly also race, a block of between two and six weeks can really give you a jump in power, and can be used effectively in tapering for a major event.

Training with heart rate

Heart rate monitors have been around for years and yet there are still many cyclists who don't know how to use them properly. But why train using heart rate as a guide at all? Elite cyclists now use a combination of heart rate monitors and power meters to gauge their training intensity. Power meters are all the rage at the moment, but for the average rider a heart rate monitor is still the best training tool you can buy.

Heart rate gives a direct indication of the level of stress placed on the body at any given time. For around £40, you can get a monitor that is accurate enough to enable the athlete to indicate changes in fitness and even the onset of overtraining or illness. But its most important function is its ability to determine training intensity. It will enable you to make the best use of the time you have available to train.

Choosing a heart rate monitor

Polar, the originator of the commercially available heart rate monitor, is still considered to be the market leader, but there are many other manufacturers who make good-quality heart rate monitors. It is possible to pay more than £250 for a monitor that will allow you to download data and will come with a highly technical software package adequate for the use of an Olympic athlete and their coach or physiologist. However, for the average rider it is really not necessary to buy such an expensive monitor; you may never gain the full benefit of the functions it offers.

All you need is a good-quality monitor that is accurate and allows you to set upper and lower heart rate limits. Such a monitor will feature alarms that sound when your heart rate goes higher or lower than the limits you have set. This is important because you don't want to be riding around having to look at your heart rate monitor display all the time. As long as you can attach the heart rate monitor to the handlebars on your bike, that is about all you need it to do.

So a basic monitor will suffice, but if you are prepared to pay a little more there are functions that are desirable, but not essential. A monitor that allows data to be recorded at the end of a session means you can log your average heart rate and maybe the amount of calories burned during your ride. This data can be useful to assess how your fitness is improving and to help you lose weight.

Determining maximum heart rate

Before any scientific training programme can begin, the physiologist or self-coached athlete must first determine the current state of fitness. Ideally such an assessment would be carried out using a selection of physiological tests in a recognised sports laboratory. We have included a section on the benefits of physiological testing later in this chapter. But we realise that not everyone reading this book will have the opportunity to undergo such a test. Therefore, we need to find another way of testing that, although not as accurate as a laboratory test, will provide data on which to base a scientific training programme. At the very least, we need

to find out the athlete's maximum heart rate through a physical test. Many books recommend theoretical formulae for calculating maximum heart rate based on the athlete's age but these can be wildly inaccurate. So we will ask you to carry out your own test.

Whether the test takes place in a sports science lab or is self-administered, it is hard work for the athlete. It involves an all-out effort, so there are a few things to consider before proceeding.

For a healthy, injury-free individual the maximum heart rate test is perfectly safe. However, if you have health problems (for example, if you or members of your family have a history of heart problems), or are returning to exercise after a long period of inactivity, you should check with your GP before proceeding. If you are fit and healthy and are a regular cyclist, the test will be no more demanding than a hard training ride or sportive event. Due to motivational factors associated with riding an event with or against other riders, individuals will sometimes find the maximum heart rates they achieve out on the road during an event are higher than those they reach in a structured test.

Having dealt with the health advice before taking the test, there are some other factors to consider to ensure we get the most accurate result possible. Before taking the maximum heart rate test the athlete must:

- be in a rested condition: preferably in the same rested condition as they would be prior to a big race. Ideally, testing should take place at least 48 hours after the last bout of heavy training;

- be fully hydrated and have a good level of carbohydrate stores;
- have performed a warm-up;
- use their usual training or competition equipment.

So, if you are healthy and injury free, and have heeded the advice above, you can think about taking the test.

The test is best performed using your racing bike on a stationary turbo trainer. You will need a turbo trainer with a speedometer, or a bike with a speedometer that works with the turbo trainer. Most bike speedometers operate using a sensor on the front wheel, whereas turbos are generally designed to accommodate a bike with the front wheel removed. Most decent-quality turbo trainers have speedometers in any case.

On the road, the effects of wind chill will help dissipate heat. But when you are on a stationary trainer heat builds up, causing excessive sweating. This causes the heart to beat faster and can affect the result of the test, so if working on a turbo trainer get a fan to keep you cool.

You will also need to be wearing your heart rate monitor and to check that it is picking up your heart beat before starting. Ideally, your monitor will have a record function that will allow you to view data from the test when it is over. Remember, you need to find your maximum

heart rate, so make sure your heart rate monitor records this data. If it does not, you will have to strap the heart rate monitor to your handlebars and watch it to see the highest figure achieved. Better still, get a friend to keep an eye on it while you concentrate on riding.

Perform an easy warm-up, spinning low gears for around 15 minutes, and make sure the cooling fan is on. Start the test riding at your normal pedalling cadence (the number of pedal revolutions per minute). Begin by riding at around 25 km/h (15 mph) and increase this by 1 km/h (0.6 mph) every 30 seconds. To save you looking at a stopwatch all the time, it's best to get a watch with a repeat countdown timer set to sound an alarm every 30 seconds. As each 30 seconds passes and you increase your speed, you will also have to increase your cadence or move up to a higher gear.

The idea is to continue this until the workload becomes so great that you can no longer continue increasing speed. At this point, your heart should be working at its maximum and the test is complete. You can now warm down by shifting to a low gear and gently spinning for 10 to 15 minutes.

While the main objective of this test is to determine maximum heart rate, you can also record the maximum speed achieved during the test. If in future months you perform the same test with exactly the same bike and turbo trainer set-up, you can use it to identify improvements in fitness.

The benefits of physiological testing

Figure 7.5 Testing cyclists at Sportstest

The test to determine your maximum heart rate will allow you to target your training and measure the intensity of your sessions on the bike. It is a scientific approach that will bring benefits and help you make the most of the time you have available to train. However there are things that the maximum heart rate test will not do.

While the method we have outlined is a good place to start, there are advantages to be had from undergoing a full physiological assessment at a reputable sports science laboratory. Physiological tests can help to optimise training and enhance performance. Testing gives you an indication of your current physiological status, outlining your strengths and weaknesses. Repeat testing allows you to monitor your progress. Performance in training and competition can indicate how well an athlete

performs, but not the reasons why. To get the most from the tests, it is important to use medically accurate apparatus and sports-specific scientific methods to assess why you are performing as you are (Figure 7.5), allowing you and/or your coach to adjust your training programmes accordingly.

Ideally, fitness testing sessions should include assessment of body fat. Knowing body fat percentage is helpful in setting nutritional targets (including carbohydrate, protein and fat intakes) to aid weight loss (where required), or enhance recovery from training. Then cycling-specific test protocols enable assessment of fitness by measuring maximal oxygen uptake (VO_2max), maximum heart rate, heart rate training zones, peak power output, power-to-weight ratios, anaerobic threshold, and sub-maximal VO_2 to determine economy or efficiency.

In addition to standard testing services, biomechanical and psychological support and intervention can also be provided if this is a key weakness in your performance. Up until a few years ago, all of this was only available to an elite few on Olympic programmes or professional teams. You can still make significant performance gains without physiological testing if you follow the guidelines in this book. But if you want to achieve the best possible performance, a full physiological assessment would be a good place to start.

What the numbers mean

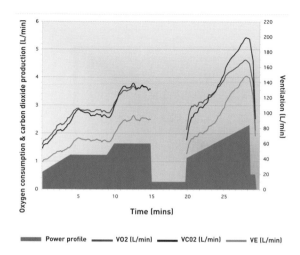

Figure 7.6 Results of a fitness assessment

Figure 7.6 shows the results of a fitness assessment undertaken at Sportstest. The first 15-minute period of the assessment is a sub-maximal test. Following a period of four minutes of increasing intensity, workloads were selected to reflect the rider's weight and ability. It would be expected that a trained rider would undertake aerobic training at a power approximating 3 Watts per kg body mass, and would be close to threshold at a workload of 4 Watts per kg. In both cases, these workloads are maintained for five minutes to allow a steady state to be achieved.

Oxygen uptake (the blue line) was measured continuously throughout the sub-maximal test. The primary value of these measures is to monitor changes with training; however, they are also used to determine efficiency and fuel utilisation rate. Put simply, oxygen consumed

will be converted to energy, and the percentage of this energy that is being used to produce power (as opposed to being dissipated as heat, or used to keep the body upright) can be determined. A well-trained, elite rider would be expected to be 24 or 25 per cent efficient. Values lower than this are caused by either poor metabolic processes or poor biomechanics.

After a further five-minute rest period, a progressive maximal test is undertaken. Workloads are designed to gradually increase at a rate suitable for the individual rider's ability. Again, breathing is monitored throughout and, as the workload is increased, the graph shows the linear increase in oxygen uptake (VO_2) as a blue line. The waste gas carbon dioxide (VCO_2) is also monitored and its production is illustrated as a red line.

Significantly, where the rider is working aerobically, and able to use both fat and carbohydrate as a fuel, the blue line (VO_2) will be above the red line (VCO_2). The point of threshold occurs when the two lines come together; this also represents the use of 100 per cent carbohydrate as a fuel. Where the red line (VCO_2) is above the blue (VO_2), this demonstrates that the rider is working anaerobically to maintain the load. In some cases it can take several minutes to reach equilibrium, hence the values at the end of each steady period are observed in the sub-maximal test.

The results of these and similar tests can then be used to determine training zones which are far more specific to your current fitness and individual heart rate responses.

The training zones

The results of laboratory testing will allow accurate determination of heart rate for specific zones. However, if you have a self-tested maximum heart rate, using this figure we can predict heart rate training zones to develop different areas of fitness. We will be working with training zones that are based on principles established by Peter Keen and later adopted by the British cycling team. Some coaches and physiologists use six or seven zones, but the principles of training specific muscle groups for a particular purpose remain the same.

Let's take a look at the five training zones (or levels) we shall use to explain the physiological approach to our training programme.

Recovery/base (R&B) training <149

Steady-state, long-distance rides of very low intensity. Rides at this intensity could be maintained for five hours or more. The limiting factors are adequate supplies of fluid and carbohydrate, or energy from fat stores.

In training for sportive rides or other endurance events, rides at this low intensity are only of real use in getting the body used to being on a bike for long periods. Such low-intensity riding is the type many cyclists have used for years, believing that 'getting the miles in' was the only way to

achieve optimum fitness. Such a traditional, non-scientific approach was based on the belief that more was better. If 600 km (about 375 miles) a week was followed by a race win, then 1000 km (approximately 600 miles) a week would produce even better results!

Of course, we now know that such a system may allow some riders to perform well, but most will end up overtrained and fatigued. Rides at this intensity in our training programme will be used to allow riders to adapt to long hours on the bike and, in much shorter rides, to allow for recovery from a heavy training session. As a guide, rides at this level should be performed at heart rates at least 45 beats per minute (bpm) below your maximum. So if your maximum is 190 bpm, you should not exceed 145 at this level.

Endurance (END) training $149 - 159$

This is the key session in your programme. You will do more endurance work than any other in order to optimise your performance. Endurance training rides are significantly more intense than the recovery/base training level, but are not 'flat out' efforts. You should experience the sort of feeling you would during a steady ride, certainly much easier than you would feel during a time trial or hill climb. If you were riding with a group you would have to concentrate on your pace, and would be able to have a conversation with another rider, *but* you'd need to take a deep and full breath, probably between each sentence. If the conversation becomes free flowing, you are riding too easily. If the ride pace increases so that you can no longer maintain the conversation, you are probably riding too hard. Sessions at this intensity need only last for an hour, although ideally they will be between 90 minutes and two hours.

It is possible to train at this intensity for longer, but the potential muscle damage caused by doing so outweighs any extra benefits gained. The idea is to be able to stress the body enough to prompt a training response, without causing so much fatigue that it takes two or three days to recover sufficiently to be able to resume training at the same intensity.

Endurance training is important because it promotes significant improvements in both cardiovascular and energy efficiency. These sessions require significant amounts of carbohydrate, so carbohydrate drinks or gels must be used. This level of training uses the slow-twitch (type 1) aerobic muscle fibre that it's vital to train for improved endurance. Essentially it is a fat-burning fibre, although in endurance training sessions you will be using a significant amount of carbohydrate too. If you are predicting your training zones from your maximum heart rate, rides at this level should be done between 35 to 45 bpm below your maximum. So if your maximum heart rate is 190, you should ride at between 145 and 155 bpm.

Mixed muscle zone (MMZ) training

This is a zone in between the endurance zone and threshold zone. Our research suggests that the MMZ uses a mix of the slow (type 1) and fast-twitch aerobic (type 2a) muscle fibres used in those two zones. Our training programme will not target training in this zone, because it is not going to produce the specific benefits needed to improve your performance for sportive riding, especially when you have limited training time. We mention this zone because it is commonly the zone in which many riders ending up training.

Training in this zone will bring some fitness benefits, but they will not be as rapid as the benefits of targeted training in the endurance and threshold zones. This mixed muscle zone will fatigue both endurance type 1 muscle fibres and threshold type 2a muscle fibres. One of the advantages of targeting endurance and threshold fibres on separate days is that it allows the muscle fibres more opportunity to recover between training sessions, an opportunity that is lost by training in this zone. When training in the endurance zone, the muscle fibres used for threshold training are getting a chance to recover and vice versa. This is especially important if you think back to Figure 7.3, showing the impact of training overload and recovery.

Threshold (ThT) training   169 – 179

Sessions at this intensity are important for the sportive rider because they will improve climbing ability. Threshold sessions are at an intensity on a par with a 40 km (25 miles) time-trial effort. They can be performed on the flat, but ideally you will have a climb long enough for you to do them all uphill. Alternatively, you could use a turbo trainer. These sessions will be continuous efforts of between 20 and 40 minutes, or extending interval repetitions of between 3 and 12 minutes. They will improve your lactic acid tolerance and enable you to sustain greater power outputs on long climbs.

This level of effort involves the fast-twitch oxidative (type 2a) muscle fibres, which require large amounts of oxygen to function properly. The sensation a rider should have at this intensity is of a hard, but not flat-out, effort. Your breathing should be rhythmical and deep and you would not be able to hold a conversation. You should be able to respond to a question with a one- or two-word answer, but that's about all. Rides at this level should be done between an estimated 15 to 25 bpm below your maximum heart rate. So if your maximum heart rate is 190, you should ride at between 165 and 175 bpm.

Speed and power (S&P) training   (79+

This is the icing on the cake. Short, high-intensity interval training designed to provide the finishing touches to your training in the final weeks before a big event. Such sessions involve maximum effort, with relatively long recovery periods.

Because sportive rides are essentially endurance events in which the individual is aiming to complete the ride in the fastest time possible, rather than trying to win a sprint at the end of a long ride, maximal or interval training is not that important. But a few weeks of training that includes this type of session can produce benefits that may help you close a gap to catch a group of riders, or give you the power to accelerate out of slow hairpin bends on a descent.

This type of effort involves the use of the fast-twitch, glycolytic (type 2b) muscle fibres, which do not require the use of oxygen to function. They come into play in a sprint or when the athlete is fatigued and simply cannot take in oxygen quickly enough to supply anaerobic muscle fibres. Type 2b fibres cause a large increase in lactic acid production, leading to rapid onset of fatigue. When riding at this level you should be attaining a heart rate no more than 15 bpm below your maximum. So if your maximum heart rate is 190 bpm, you should ride above 175 bpm, although heart rate is not the critical issue here: you should look to apply maximum effort when doing these sessions.

Training effectively

It is vitally important that in each session you try to maintain your heart rate within the specified training zones. For example, if your endurance zone heart rate is from 145 to 155 bpm, you must set the limits on your heart monitor to alert you when you are moving in and out of this zone.

Some heart rate monitors will tell you what your average heart rate was at the end of a training ride. This can be misleading. For instance, say you had an average heart rate reading of 150 bpm after an hour-long training ride. This would seem fine if you had a heart rate range of 145–155 bpm for an endurance session. But if you spent the first 30 minutes exercising at 130 bpm and the last 30 minutes at 170 bpm, you would have spent virtually no time at all in the specified zone. Your aim should be to spend as much of your training session as possible within your recommended zone.

Out on the road, your heart rate will vary due to terrain or having to stop at traffic lights and so on. As the terrain changes, you should adjust your gearing and pedalling speed to keep your heart rate at the right level. So on an endurance ride, that means gearing down when you get to a steep hill, and using a faster cadence or higher gears on a descent. If you have to stop at traffic lights or a junction, you should aim to accelerate gradually until your heart rate increases and it is back within the target zone.

Remember, the key to this training programme is that it targets specific muscle groups to gain specific physiological benefits.

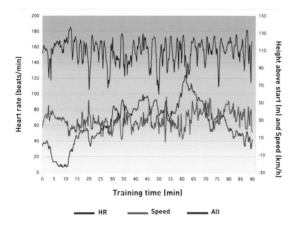

Figure 7.7 Heart rate response of a rider in group training

If you are on an endurance ride and your heart rate drops too low, there is no point in sprinting away to get it back up into the target zone. Doing that will involve using the type 2b

fast-twitch sprint fibres. This interrupts the stress being placed on the endurance fibres and it may take the body 15 or 20 minutes to clear the anaerobic backlog and bring the endurance fibres back into most effective use. If you constantly switch between using different types of muscle fibres, you will not initiate the physiological changes we want to promote for improved fitness.

Figure 7.7 shows a classic example of a rider training within a group environment. As can be clearly seen, there are massive fluctuations in heart rate response. While this rider maintains his objective of averaging between 150 and 160 bpm for the duration of the ninety-minute ride the red bars in Figure 7.9 show the distribution of the heart rate over the training session. Only around 30 per cent of the session was spent in the correct training zone. That's 70 per cent of the session wasted, or where the rider could have been working more effectively, or doing other things.

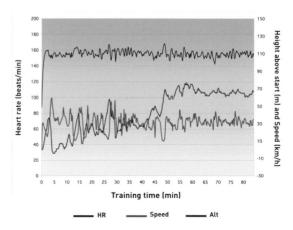

Figure 7.8 The ideal riding approach

Figure 7.8 shows the riding approach we are advocating. It is not easy to achieve, but in this case the rider spends over 80 per cent of time in the correct training zone. This is achieved by decreasing pace on climbs, and working hard on descents. This makes the ride far more effective. It also means that, if we again consider the principle of training overload (see Figure 7.3), the rider can work in a different intensity zone on the next training ride, thereby maximising the recovery time of the particular group of muscle fibres recruited in the training.

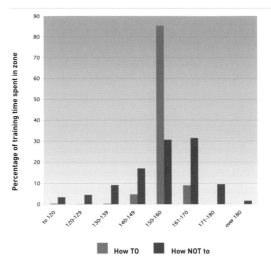

Figure 7.9 Illustrates the structured nature of working within a heart rate zone. The blue bars show the time in each training zone from the riders' data using the focused training approach (Figure 7.8), whereas the red bars show the wider spread of heart rates from group or unstructured training (Figure 7.7)

8

BUILDING A TRAINING PROGRAMME

Your training programme is something that you plan many months in advance of a major race. It is virtually impossible to set out a programme lasting six or eight months and be able to perform every session as planned. Indeed, it would be misguided to force yourself to follow such a programme because it would mean ignoring signs of overtraining and would probably lead to illness or injury. The point of building a training programme is to create a guide aimed at bringing you to peak condition for your chosen event.

The training programme then is not a template to be followed blindly, but more the framework of a jigsaw into which you will fit the pieces over the coming months. After each week of your programme, you should give time to assess how

you have performed and be ready to alter your next week's schedule accordingly. We have set out three training plan structures for you to adapt to your own circumstances. The three programmes are for a novice sportive rider, an experienced rider and an advanced rider. They are devised by taking the date of your big race and working backwards to where you are now. We shall assume that the big race is in July, with your training beginning in October. The actual dates we use are not important; it is the methodology behind the creation of the programme that is vital.

All the training that we propose is based upon time spent on the bike rather than the distance covered, and requires you to use the training zones, or training sensations, described in the previous chapter. This means that, as your fitness increases, the intensity you work at will remain appropriate to your physiology, and your ride speed should gradually improve. Be warned, however, that these are just guidelines to set your training targets. You will not achieve your potential by always doing the minimum suggested.

The novice rider

The novice rider is one that has little or no cycling background, or one who has done some cycle training or racing, but not tackled a long-distance sportive event before. For the novice rider attempting their first big sportive event, we shall assume that their aim is to finish (or finish within an allotted time if it is an event like the Étape du Tour that has time limits).

Table 8.1 October to December – Base endurance/build phase		
Phase duration	One to three months ideally	
Training time	4–8 hrs per week	
Aim	This phase is about getting you to spend more time on the bike and to get used to training regularly	
Day	Activity	Time
Monday	Rest	
Tuesday	END zone	45–90 mins
Wednesday	Rest or R&B zone	20–30 mins as recovery ride
Thursday	END zone	45–90 mins
Friday	Rest	
Saturday	END zone	60–90 mins
Sunday	Unstructured easy ride. Don't worry about your training intensity; enjoy the time on your bike.	60–180 mins

You should aim to build up the time spent on the bike in three-week cycles. Start off with a level of training you are comfortable with, then aim to add time to sessions the next week. The third week in the cycle should be a recovery week in which you reduce the volume of training to less than the first week in the cycle. In this way, you give your body time to regenerate and adapt to the increased stress being placed upon it.

Table 8.2 January to April – Base endurance phase

Phase duration	12–16 week training block	
Training time	6–12 hrs per week	
Aim	To build up volume of endurance riding	
Day	Activity	Time
Monday	Rest	
Tuesday	END zone	90–120 mins
Wednesday	Rest or R&B zone	20–30 mins
Thursday	END zone	90–120 mins
Friday	Rest	
Saturday	END zone	90–120 mins
Sunday	Long *continuous* steady ride in R&B zone	2–6 hrs

Table 8.3 April to July – Transition phase

Phase duration	Eight-week threshold training block to start 10 weeks before race day	
Training time	8–14 per week	
Aim	To build on endurance base and introduce threshold sessions. Volume decreases but intensity increases. Threshold sessions aimed at improving climbing ability	
Day	**Activity**	**Time**
Monday	Rest	
Tuesday	ThT zone	sessions as below
Wednesday	END zone	60–120 mins
Thursday	ThT zone	sessions as below
Friday	Rest	
Saturday	ThT zone	sessions as below
Sunday	END or R&B ride	3–8 hrs

Note: Threshold sessions can be:

- Two or three efforts of 12 mins, with 8 mins recovery; or:
- Between three and five efforts of 8 mins, with 6 mins recovery; or:
- Between four and eight efforts of 5 mins with 3 mins recovery.

Additionally, threshold sessions should include a warm-up and warm-down period of between 10 and 30 minutes.

Table 8.4 Taper phase

Phase duration	Two weeks before event	
Training time	3–6 per week	
Aim	To allow full recovery prior to race day and also to use short, high-intensity sessions to build more power	
Day	**Activity**	**Time**
Monday	Rest	
Tuesday	S&P hill efforts	4–6 seated efforts, in a big gear, of 20–30 sec, with 5 mins recovery
Wednesday	Rest or R&B zone ride	30 mins
Thursday	S&P session	three efforts of 3 mins maximum effort with 3 mins recovery
Friday	Rest	
Saturday	ThT session	of two or three efforts of 8 mins with two mins recovery
Sunday	END zone ride	90–120 mins

During the final week before race day, you should reduce this workload even further, with nothing but easy recovery rides in the last three days before the race.

The experienced rider

The experienced rider is one who has from three to six years of regular cycle training or racing. They may already have completed a sportive ride of the type and distance they intend to train for now. Their aim will be to improve their performance, maybe having already achieved bronze standard in the Étape du Tour and aiming for a silver medal or better next time. Assuming they are regular cyclists who may have spent a season racing, the month of October can be treated as a rest period. Training for a sportive in July begins in November with a month-long build phase of base riding.

Table 8.5 November to March – base volume training		
Phase duration	Minimum of three months	
Training time	8–18 hrs per week	
Aim	To build up volume of endurance work	
Day	**Activity**	**Time**
Monday	Rest	
Tuesday	END zone	90–120 mins
Wednesday	ThT session, or R&B or rest	30–60 mins
Thursday	END zone	90–120 mins
Friday	Rest or R&B zone	60–120 mins
Saturday	END zone	60–240 mins
Sunday	Unstructured easy ride or club run	2–6 hrs

This phase should be based on a four-week cycle, with three weeks of adding volume followed by a recovery week. If you feel capable of coping with more, you can introduce a 'crash' week on the third week of the build phase, where you put in a really tough workout before the rest week. This accentuates the training response caused by the excessive overload, but there are risks involved. Crash weeks put a lot of strain on the body and may temporarily weaken your immune system, leaving you susceptible to colds or viruses. So extra attention must be paid to nutrition and recovery between sessions during these crash weeks.

Table 8.6 April to June – threshold training

Phase duration	8–12 weeks, to continue until 2 weeks pre-event	
Training time	4–12 hours per week	
Aim	To introduce threshold training sessions to improve climbing ability	
Day	Activity	Time
Monday	Rest	
Tuesday	ThT as below, *or* END zone	45–60 mins
Wednesday	END zone	90–180 mins
Thursday	ThT session as below	
Friday	R&B zone	45–60 mins
Saturday	ThT session as below	
Sunday	Long ride	2–6 hrs

Note: Threshold sessions can be any one of the following:

- A 16–40 km (10–25 mile) time trial.
- Between two and four efforts of 12 mins with 3 mins recovery.
- Between three and five efforts of 8 mins with 2 mins recovery.
- Between four and eight efforts of 5 mins with 1 min recovery.

All sessions should include a warm-up and cool-down phase lasting ideally 15–30 mins. Additionally, over the weeks you can introduce some power sessions. Replace one or more of the threshold sessions with a power session. Suggested power workouts can be from three to six efforts of three minutes at maximum effort with three minutes recovery.

Table 8.7 June/July – taper

Phase duration	Two-week taper phase starting two weeks before race day	
Training time	4–8 per week	
Aim	To allow the athlete to recover and ensure peak fitness on race day	
Day	**Activity**	**Time**
Monday	Rest	
Tuesday	S&P session	6 x 30 sec sprints with 5 mins recovery
Wednesday	R&B zone	45 mins recovery ride
Thursday	S&P session	4 x 30 sec hill efforts with 5 minutes recovery
Friday	Rest or R&B zone ride	45–60 mins
Saturday	ThT effort	4 x 5 mins, 1 min rest
Sunday	END zone	90–180 mins

During the final week before race day, you should reduce this workload even further, with nothing but easy recovery rides in the last three days before the race.

The advanced rider

The advanced rider is one that has a solid racing background and several years of training and competition. Their aim will be to improve on previous performances and they will be prepared to commit more time to training than those in the novice and experienced categories. As we would expect the advanced rider to have spent most of the summer racing, it is reasonable for the months of October and November to be treated as a recovery period with just easy, unstructured riding taking place. We shall assume that the focus of the rider's forthcoming season will be a long-distance sportive ride in July.

Table 8.8 December to March – base volume training

Phase duration	Ideally a minimum of three months		
Training time	10–22 hrs per week		
Aim	To build cardiovascular base fitness and improve endurance capacity		
Day		Activity	Time
Monday		Rest	
Tuesday	am pm	R&B zone ride END zone	30–60 mins 120–180 mins
Wednesday	am pm	R&B zone Rest or R&B zone	30–120 mins 20–60 mins
Thursday	am pm	R&B zone ride END zone	30–60 mins 2–4 hrs
Friday		R&B zone recovery	30–60 mins
Saturday		END zone	2–4 hrs
Sunday		club run – unstructured ride	3–5 hrs

Because the advanced rider may be undertaking a reasonably high volume of training, it may be necessary to carry out two training sessions on some days. But always remember that it is not an aim to clock up as many hours as you can. Always be conscious of how you are recovering between sessions and adjust your training accordingly.

Table 8.9 April to June – threshold training block

Phase duration	10–12 weeks, to continue until two weeks before race day	
Training time	16–18 per week	
Aim	To introduce threshold training sessions to improve climbing ability	
Day	Activity	Time
Monday	Rest or ThT session	six–eight efforts of 5 mins with 1 min recovery
Tuesday	R&B zone	45–90 mins
Wednesday	END zone	3–5 hrs
Thursday	S&P session	hills, flat sprints or sustained efforts of 3 mins, all with 3–5 mins full recovery
Friday	Rest	
Saturday	am: END zone pm: ThT session	90–120 mins as below
Sunday	Long ride, either END zone ride or unstructured club run	2–6 hrs

Figure 8.1 A time trial can be a useful training session for a sportive rider, or a logical step into bike racing

Alternative threshold sessions can be any one of the following:

- A time trial of 16 40 km (10 25 miles).
- Between two and four efforts of 12 mins with 3 mins recovery.
- Between three and five efforts of 8 mins with 2 mins recovery.
- Between four and eight efforts of 5 mins with 1 min recovery.

Monday and Tuesday could also be swapped dependant on recovery from the weekend. The experienced rider may also wish to add a second light session on some training days. These sessions should be performed with a warm-up and warm-down of a minimum of 15 mins, but possibly as long as 45 mins.

Adapting the training programme for other types of riding

This book has focused on training and preparation for long-distance sportive events. But there are other types of both on- and off-road riding out there that many of you may be interested in taking part in. Essentially this book is about giving you the knowledge to be able to coach yourself, so it should be quite easy for you to take the training principles we have set out and adapt them to other events. Although the structure of your training programme will change, the basic principles remain the same. The importance of recovery, of training within your specified training zones and of paying attention to nutrition are all the same. In this section we shall give a few pointers for those of you wanting to take part in some of the most popular forms of road racing after sportive riding – time-trialling and criterium or circuit racing. We will also provide some suggestions if you want to look at non-competitive events such as charity or audax rides.

Time-trialling

A time trial is known as the 'race of truth' because it is about the rider competing alone against the clock. There are no great tactical aspects to the time trial: it's all about who can ride the fastest over a given distance. The most popular time trial events tend to be between 16 km (10 miles) and 40 km (25 miles). There are also stage race events that involve a time trial stage combined with road race stages.

For the time-triallist, the main focus of training will be threshold work to build up resistance to fatigue and to train the muscle fibres that will allow you to ride at your threshold intensity for as long as possible. To outline a time-trialling training programme, we shall assume that the competitive season ends in September and begins again in April or May.

As with the sportive programme, the time-triallist's training will begin in October with around 12 to 16 weeks of base endurance work, with the individual putting in as many endurance sessions as time will allow. These would be sessions of between one and two hours. If you are not intending to ride any events over 40 km (25 miles), there is no need to undertake base endurance rides of more than two or three hours. This training block is then followed by a block lasting from 10 to 12 weeks in which threshold sessions are introduced in a similar way to the sportive programmes we have outlined.

A two-week taper before a big race should be used, but without the speed and power sessions because time-trialling, unlike road racing, does not involve any sudden accelerations. If you are competing in a series of time trials over a period of weeks, your fitness can be maintained by racing with threshold sessions in between. As with the other training programmes, it is advisable to build in recovery weeks after a period of competition or hard training. It is important to make your training as specific as possible to the event you will be competing in, so whenever possible you should ride using your time trial bike with aero bars.

Criterium/circuit racing

Criterium races tend to be made up of laps of a short road circuit of around 1 or 2 km (approximately 1 mile), with events lasting around one hour. As the races usually involve racing around tight circuits, the rider will have to train to cope with constant accelerations out of corners and to get used to being able to jump away from a group, or chase down riders who have broken clear.

Typically, the criterium racer's programme will be similar to the sportive programme and will be dependent on the experience level of the individual. A two-week taper before a major race is advisable, but these two weeks should be preceded by between four and eight weeks of training with an emphasis on speed and power to cope with the high-intensity efforts of the event.

For the sportive rider, this may mean a local road race, or a sportive ride that can provide good training, as well as a means of assessing how your form is progressing. It can also be good for morale if you complete a race or ride and feel that your performance in relation to others is improving.

Charity rides and audax events

Not every rider has a competitive desire. Maybe you are just looking to ride your bike for enjoyment, fitness, and possibly health

TIPS FROM THE TOP
Getting and keeping motivated

Once you have set a long-term goal like riding the Étape du Tour, it is important to set more immediate goals too, says pro rider Mark Cavendish. 'You have your big goal at the top, but you have to have little goals along the way,' he says. It is difficult for many riders to stay focused and motivated for an event that is six or eight months away. Creating medium- and short-term goals is a way of maintaining motivation. If you can keep telling yourself that you just need to keep training until you reach the short-term goal of a race in a few weeks, it's easier to stay motivated than it would be if your only goal was six months down the line.

'You have to focus on the purpose behind the training,' says Great Britain Olympic Academy rider Jonny Bellis, who won bronze in the 2007 World Championship under-23 road race. 'There's no point doing it for no reason, so you have to concentrate on why you are training.' Bellis also believes in the importance of setting intermediate and short-term goals to help the rider stay motivated for training. 'You can pick a race two weeks down the line and train towards that,' he says. 'It's just a case of seeing how you get on there and then looking at how you need to improve.'

reasons. All these are perfectly valid and acceptable reasons to get out on your bike. But you may well gain a greater sense of enjoyment by sharing your pastime with others. If you fit into this category, you will possibly want to alter the training recommendations to better suit your needs.

The key target of most charity rides, audax events or randonnées, is to complete a set distance or route within a reasonably generous time goal. You will often be able to stop and take breaks whenever you wish, and for as long as you want. The nature of this riding therefore becomes a lot more focused on the ability to cope with the distance of the event you have chosen, and many of the higher intensity aspects of competitive riding, or sportive riding, can be omitted from your training programme.

For example, although the ability to 'hold a wheel' or 'draft' other riders is a useful skill, these rides will usually be undertaken with a group that is working together, rather than competing against each other. So the workload will often be shared, and the high power needed to ride away from other riders will not be of benefit. Therefore, high-intensity speed and power intervals need not be included in planned sessions. Similarly, extended intervals or threshold sessions may only be of value to the charity or audax rider if the event includes a number of potentially stressful climbs.

Finally, and depending on the demands of the event, the total training needed should be considered carefully. Obviously, many weeks of carefully planned training would be needed for an attempt at a 400 or 600 kilometre (248–373 miles) audax, whereas the rider doing a charity event of 40 or 50 kilometres (25–30 miles) can take a far more relaxed approach, and may only look to train three or four times per week.

9

ISSUES AND PROBLEMS WITH TRAINING

How to avoid overtraining

If Eskimos have many different words for snow, sports scientists have several different words for overtraining. As we have discussed already, the key to making improvements in your performance is not only to undertake the correct type of training session, but to also allow your body adequate time to recover afterwards.

Constantly pushing your body too hard in training is certain to cause excessive fatigue, which will disrupt your training as you have to take extended periods of rest. This is what we call overtraining, and in mild cases it will just be a case of having a few days rest to recover from a particularly hard period of training. In extreme cases, it can cause your immune system to be suppressed and leave you vulnerable to virus infections that may have long-term implications for your health. So it is important to be aware of the causes and symptoms of overtraining.

Overtraining is most often caused by too much high-intensity training or a sudden increase in either the intensity or the volume of training. This is why the training programme we have set out aims to gradually increase the physical demands involved, so your body has time to adapt to the stresses being placed upon it.

Sudden increases in training intensity or training volume are to be avoided. But even if you increase your training gradually, there are other factors that may still lead to overtraining.

Too little sleep, stress at work or in your home life, or an undetected illness can all lead to overtraining symptoms. The individual has to learn to listen to their body and learn from experience to correctly identify when these symptoms are a sign of overtraining, and when they're simply a normal level of fatigue after a hard training session. Keeping track of your resting pulse rate first thing in the morning is a good way of spotting signs of overtraining (see next section).

There are six key physiological responses to training to be aware of. They will help you differentiate between what is a normal response to training and what may be the onset of overtraining:

1 **Training overload:** The training stress itself.
2 **Training fatigue/stress:** Normal fatigue associated with heavy training.
3 **Overtraining:** Training has to cause the individual so much strsss that they are unable to perform at an optimal level following an appropriate regeneration period. A drop in performance must also be experienced.
4 **Overreaching:** Follows intentional or unintentional short-term overtraining.

Symptoms can be reversed with a longer regeneration period.
5 **Overtraining syndrome:** Chronically depressed performance plus other symptoms. Significant rest is required.
6 **Overstrain:** Follows acute muscle damage by isolated intensive training. May or may not be associated with overreaching or overtraining syndrome.

Symptoms of overtraining

The symptoms of overtraining may fall into five different areas: physiological, performance-related, psychological, immunological and biochemical. An athlete may show signs of only one of these symptoms or an array. Many sports scientists suggest that the athlete's own results, rather than a comparison to a standard population, must be used to identify the subtle changes that may be indicative of the onset of overtraining.

Generally, the overtraining syndrome is a form of chronic fatigue. In the elite athlete, there may be a fragile balance between peak performance and chronic fatigue. For these athletes, as much as six weeks of full rest can be necessary to return individuals to their normal state.

Table 9.1 Common signs and symptoms of overtraining

Performance indicators	Physiological indices
• Abnormal muscle soreness or pain • Heavy legged feeling • General inability to undertake training • Drop off in performance • Reduced endurance capacity	• Increased resting heart rate • Suppressed training heart rate (for a given intensity) • Elevated post exercise heart rate • Excessive thirst • Increased night sweating
Health related signs	**Psychological**
• Abnormal fluctuations in body weight • Loss of appetite • Increased nocturnal fluid intake • General lower resistance (for example increased sore throats, mouth ulcers, common colds) • Poor healing of wounds • Disturbed sleep • Gastro-intestinal disturbances	• Generalised apathy/lethargy • Shortened attention span • Irritability • Impaired co-ordination • General loss of interest in training • Depression

Occurrence of overtraining syndrome

If we reconsider the model of training overload (see Figure 7.3 on page 67), it is easy to understand how overtraining syndrome develops, and occurs in three different phases:

• **Phase 1:** Following a hard training session, discomfort may be felt in the muscle and perceived exertion while exercising may increase. This is essentially the regeneration phase from points B to C. This can soon be rectified with rest.

• **Phase 2:** If the athlete persists with training, before recovery (point C) has been achieved, there will be a further decline in performance and other symptoms may develop. A few days of rest may be sufficient to prevent the progression of the syndrome.

- **Phase 3:** If the athlete continues to train without adequate rest (thereby repeating phases 1 and 2), full-blown over-training syndrome may occur. Other external stresses (for example, relating to the athlete's nutrition, environment, sleep, work and so on) could stimulate this.

While the exact mechanism and underlying causes of overtraining are not fully known, there are ways of avoiding it happening in the first place. The basic principles of training must be adhered to:

- Use heart rate to gauge training intensity.
- Use a training diary (to record diet, training, mood and so on).
- Continually review training responses.
- Use an interesting and continually changing training programme.
- Undertake physiological and, where necessary, psychological assessment.
- Implement correct nutritional practices.
- Where possible, remove other external sources of stress.

Treatment of overtraining syndrome

In order to treat overtraining, rest is key. It is vital to reduce or stop training, and minimise the previously described risks. Once sufficient rest to recover from all of the associated symptoms has been taken, training should recommence slowly and cautiously, with additional rest being taken in the early stages. The use of tapers may prove effective for the elite athlete to ensure full recovery prior to major competitions.

Using resting heart rate to identify overtraining

Your heart rate monitor is not just a vital tool in monitoring the intensity of your training sessions. It can also be used to indicate the early signs of overtraining.

The best time to take your resting heart rate is first thing in the morning when you wake up. It is possible to take it at other times during the day, but it's easiest first thing in the morning when you're at your most rested.

Taking your resting heart rate may seem like another chore to be added to an already demanding training regime, but it really is worth taking the time to do it. It is the best and easiest way of determining whether you have recovered sufficiently from your last race or hard training session, and it takes some of the guesswork out of assessing your fatigue level.

If you are unlucky enough to suffer an illness, this will suppress your immune function and elevate your heart rate. During this time, carefully monitor your resting heart rate. However, be warned that although your resting heart rate may return to its baseline, your immune function will remain suppressed for a further four or five days. You should be careful not to overtrain at this time and instead allow your body time to recover. If you don't, further and possibly more severe illness may result.

HOW TO TAKE YOUR RESTING HEART RATE

Before you go to bed, set your alarm 15 minutes earlier than normal and have your heart rate monitor next to the bed. When your alarm sounds, roll over, put on your monitor strap and start recording your heart rate. Set your alarm to snooze for 15 minutes so you can effectively record your resting heart rate. Now lie back and relax for the full 15 minutes.

Once you have completed the 'snooze test', download your heart rates from the monitor and check for the lowest average minute. This is your resting heart rate reading. If your heart rate monitor does not record your heart rate in this way, note down the average heart rate over the 15 minutes.

Whatever method you use, just make sure you stick to it each time you check your resting heart rate. You really need to check this at least once and possibly twice a week. Initially it is best to do this the day after a rest day, when you are fully recovered. For example, if you trained on Sunday and Monday is your rest day, you need to do the test on the Tuesday morning, ideally 36–48 hours after your last training session.

Once you have this fully recovered heart rate reading, you can use it to highlight days when you are still fatigued. If you wake up not feeling 100 per cent, and your heart rate monitor gives a reading that is more than five beats above your normal baseline, this is an indication that you may need to take things easy, or maybe not train at all that day.

As your training progresses, your 'fully rested' heart rate should decrease. A reduced resting heart rate is a good indicator of improved fitness in the endurance athlete. The average resting heart rate for a sedentary adult will be around 70–75 beats per minute (bpm). Elite cyclists usually have resting heart rates of 40 bpm or below; five-time Tour de France winner Miguel Indurain had a resting heart rate of 28 bpm!

As you get fitter, it is worth checking your 'fully rested' heart rate every month to six weeks. A reduction in the rate will be more noticeable in those who have only recently taken up a regular endurance training programme. More experienced athletes will not notice their resting heart rate changing that quickly.

Fitness and female riders

Elite cyclists like women's Tour de France winner Nicole Cooke will outperform 95 per cent of male cyclists in a road race. Likewise, runners like women's marathon world record holder Paula Radcliffe will be faster than all but a few elite male runners. Indeed, when Radcliffe won the World Championship marathon in Helsinki in 2005, her winning time was two minutes quicker than that of distance-running legend Emil Zatopek, who won the Olympic men's marathon title in the Finnish capital in 1952. In fact, there was no women's marathon at those Games or at any Olympics until 1984 because women were considered too frail to compete in an extreme endurance event. It's a sign of how far women's sport has come in the last few decades.

Elite men and women competitors are more closely matched in endurance sports than they are in power or speed events, so there is no real reason for training schedules to be different. Of course, the same rules apply for men and women. There is no point in a club-level cyclist trying to complete a training schedule set for an elite rider like Nicole Cooke, so follow the guidance in the training section that suits your own level.

There are many 'women's specific design' bikes and kit on the market, but they may be unnecessary for many women. Turn up at any road race or sportive and you will probably find that most women are on bikes designed for anyone, not specifically for women. If you are very short, it may be advisable to look at a women's specific design bike as they tend to come in smaller frame sizes. But the jury is still out on whether bikes and kit aimed at women are really necessary or just a clever marketing ploy. The important thing with bikes and kit is that they should fit the individual; if

you buy a bike that doesn't fit you properly on the strength of the makers' claim that it's specifically designed for women, it's a waste of money.

There are dietary considerations, such as making sure your food intake includes a good balance of minerals, especially iron. But a good diet is no more important for a female athlete than it is for a male athlete. Being aware of your dietary needs, and being aware of the importance of recovery, are vital for all athletes. The one additional consideration is menstrual irregularities that may result from overtraining.

Training considerations for the older rider

Many cyclists return to the sport in their forties, having stopped training or racing in their twenties due to family or work commitments. There will also be those of you who begin cycling later in life as a way of keeping fit or after being active in other sports. Whatever the reason, if you are over 35 and haven't been in regular cycle training for a while then there are some things you need to consider.

Basically, the rules for the older rider are the same as for everyone else in the sense that you must listen to your body and make sure you are following the rules about recovery. Adequate rest and adequate nutrition become even more important as you get older. Our ability to recover after hard training or racing become diminished, so more attention needs to be paid to these areas.

In terms of training, even as we get into our forties most individuals will be able to push themselves as hard in training as those much younger. Of course, training needs to be relative to the individual's ability and training load. But it is the speed at which we recover and adapt to that training that changes as we get older.

Those who were competitive in their twenties and return to the sport after a long lay-off run perhaps the greatest risk of overtraining. It is all too common for riders who haven't ridden regularly for a decade or more to go out and train just as they did all those years ago. Sadly, we just have to accept that our bodies do age and adjust our training accordingly. So pay more attention to the signs of overtraining and don't be afraid to rest when you need it.

The key is to treat your body with a little more respect than you may have done when you were younger. Listening to your body and how it responds to training is essential whatever age you are. It's an obvious point, but human nature being what it is this is something that we often do not learn until later in life. There is some sports science evidence to support the use of weight training for older riders to maintain muscle strength. On-the-bike training should always take priority, but if you have time in your schedule some weight training may be beneficial.

It's worth re-reading the section about pro rider Malcolm Elliott on page 38–39. In the 1980s and early 1990s Elliott was one of the world's top road riders, competing in the Tour de France and single day European classics. He won the sprinters jersey in the 1989 Tour of Spain, the highlight of his career before he retired. Malcolm made a comeback to pro racing at the age of 42 and was still competitive, winning races in the UK against pro riders half his age.

What's interesting about Malcolm's story is that, when he made his comeback, he didn't simply go out and train like he did during his earlier career. He changed his approach and learned from the advances in training methods that had happened since he retired from racing first time around. The moral of his story is that just because you trained in a certain way and had success in your twenties doesn't mean that the same training will be suitable for you later in life.

Coping with winter training

For those of you in warmer climes, this section may be one that you want to overlook. For readers in northern Europe or other colder parts of the world, however, read on. Most of you will be aiming for a big event in spring or summer, so the majority of your base mileage will have to be done in the winter months. There are no easy ways round it; the work has to be done and it is down to the individual to find the motivation within themselves to get out and do it.

Riding miles and miles on your own can be soul-destroying, so it is advisable to train with friends at least some of the time. Better still, find out where your local cycling club meets and go along on their regular weekend training ride. Most clubs have groups of different speeds to accommodate riders of various abilities. Winter club runs are a great way of making the miles pass more quickly and of learning the skills required to ride in a group.

Figure 9.1 Hill training

Top ten tips for getting the most out of winter club runs

1 Check your bike
Make sure your bike is in good mechanical condition and has mudguards fitted. It's about being considerate! You may not mind a wet backside, but the rider behind may feel differently about a face full of dirty water. Likewise, while everyone on the run will want to assist you, you don't want to get stuck 20 km (12 miles) from home with a broken chain, or only one gear working, and have to get a push home.

2 Carry a spare!
On wet roads it is always easy to pick up a puncture or two, so carry a couple of spares. And while we're on the subject of spares, always take along some spare energy gels. They'll help you get home if your legs 'fall off' – and the packaging can be used to patch a gash in a tyre!

3 Dress for the worst of the weather
You lose most heat through your hands, feet and head. So always wear gloves, booties and a hat. If you get too hot you can always take off a layer, but if you get too cold you are stuck! Also, it takes energy to maintain body heat in the cold. You may need all your energy to get round, so think sensibly.

4 Start with the easy group
If you are new to the club run, start with the easy group. As you get stronger and more confident, you can always move up. Often you will pick up far more about technical issues – how to hold a wheel and so on – by going with the steady group, than you will by spending the morning hanging on to the faster riders.

5 Drink well from the start of the ride
Even in the winter, it is easy to become dehydrated. Drink plenty, and from the start of the ride. Ideally, this should be an energy drink.

For more specific guidance, see the nutrition section on page 134.

6 Don't race . . .

. . . especially on the hills, or work too hard at the start. Share the workload, but consider the club run as a long steady ride to benefit your cardiovascular endurance. Racing up hills, or riding hard at the start of a long ride, will not only mean you are more likely to suffer at the end of the session (the faster you go, the more carbohydrate reserves you use), but you will be working at a rate that does not serve the aim of the ride. Riding through and off (that's when a group of riders help share the pace by taking it in turns riding on the front of the group) will not only help conserve your energy when you are sitting in, but this way the ride can become more social, and you learn to ride at the front, middle and back of a group.

7 Don't half-wheel

Half-wheeling is when you are on the front of a group riding with someone alongside you. Sometimes, without even being conscious of it, you may find yourself moving half a wheel ahead of the rider alongside you. The other rider then accelerates a little to keep up and the process is repeated until suddenly you are dragging the group along at 50 km/h (30 mph).

This often happens on club runs. Instead, aim to keep the pace steady. Riding too hard will only make you and everyone else suffer towards the end of the ride, and mean the purpose of the ride is lost. When you are on the front, don't take this as a chance to up the pace. Half-wheeling usually brings out the competitive nature in everyone, but often makes many suffer.

8 Record your heart rate

Use a heart rate monitor to record your progress, and help you ensure that you are working at the desired intensity (usually on a club ride it will be an indicator that you are riding too hard!). It can also serve as an early warning system if you are not drinking enough, or are running out of energy.

9 Plan a recovery strategy

Use the winter rides to develop your post-exercise recovery strategy. This should include type and timing of food intake, the need for nutritional products, stretching, and possibly a massage or bath. If you sort this out in the winter, the lessons learned will help you recover faster from races in the summer.

10 Train sensibly in the week

Put the good work you have done in the club ride to the best possible use by training sensibly in the week. Ideally this should mean riding a minimum of two or three times, with a structured approach considering both intensity and duration.

Taking the torture out of turbo training

Turbo trainers are great for enabling you to train when the weather prevents you from riding on the road, or if you are faced with riding in the dark and the increased risks that poses for cyclists. When turbo trainers first appeared in the 1980s, they tended to produce a rather 'choppy' feeling when riding. Because many turbos used fans to provide resistance, the rider often felt an uneven resistance level as they pedalled. There would often be dead spots in the pedalling action due to the turbo's mechanism.

Modern turbo trainers are better designed and allow the rider to pedal as smoothly as they can on the road. They are ideal for shorter threshold sessions because they make it easier for the rider to control their heart rate. The turbo trainer is also useful for carrying out fitness tests or assessing your maximum heart rate.

And if you are away for a few days and travelling by car, the best way to get your training in is to take your bike and a turbo trainer. A basic turbo trainer is small enough to fit into any car with plenty of room for your bike – remember, you won't even need your front wheel with some turbo trainers. With your bike and turbo in the car, you can get in that training session almost anywhere. Ideally, you would also take a fan with you to stop yourself overheating, but if this is not possible try to exercise somewhere cool or take some isotonic drinks to combat dehydration.

Some riders, however, view the turbo trainer as being like a medieval instrument of torture. The idea of spending hours in the winter sweating on the turbo fills many cyclists with horror. But the turbo trainer is an essential training tool and can be invaluable if it is used correctly. Here are some tips to make you fall in love with turbo training, rather than run away in terror.

Keep it short and sweet

It is possible to do long base endurance rides on the turbo. A five-hour ride on the turbo at the correct intensity will bring you the same fitness benefits as a similar ride on the road. But mentally this would be difficult for most people to endure: time passes much more slowly on the turbo than it does on the road. If you are mentally tough enough to cope with hours on end of turbo training, and you don't have the option of road riding, it's okay – although if you do it too much, riding with other human beings might come as a shock on race day! To prevent you dreading the thought of a turbo session, use them for shorter sessions of no more than 90 minutes.

Keep cool and stay hydrated

When you are out on the road, the wind chill created as you ride along helps to keep you cool. Riding on a stationary trainer means that heat builds up very quickly and after a few minutes the sweat will be dripping off you. Not only is this uncomfortable, but it causes your heart rate to increase due to your body trying to cool down. This affects your training heart rate, so it's best to set up a cooling fan to mimic the wind chill effect you get on the road.

Remember also that it's still necessary to keep yourself hydrated. Make sure that you use a carbohydrate drink as you would when training on the road.

Protect your bike

Even if you use a fan to keep you cool, you will still find your bike gets a shower of sweat during a turbo session. If this sweat is left on your bike over several sessions it can start to corrode metal parts, so it's best to cover the top tube and handlebar stem with a towel. If you are going to use the turbo a lot, it may even be worth setting up an old bike solely for turbo use. You don't have to have a complete bike; for most turbos, you won't need the front wheel and you can also dispense with brake calipers. But it's best to use a bike with gears to give you more control over the intensity of your ride, which will also make it easier to control your heart rate.

Get motivated

There are turbo systems with video displays that have simulated Tour de France climbs to give you a bit more motivation. You may also want to use some music or maybe Tour de France DVDs to help pass the time and get you pumped up for your training session. Some words of warning though. Riders can get carried away trying to pedal in time to the music, so it's best to avoid the techno dance stuff unless you can pedal at 200 revolutions per minute. Be careful with the DVDs too; it doesn't matter how hard you pedal, you are never going to catch Lance!

Don't become a lab rat!

Turbo trainers have their uses and are a great training tool. But there is no substitute for riding on the road. It's more fun and the training you get will be specific to what you are training for. There is no turbo trainer for the Étape du Tour. When you are riding on the road you will be constantly changing pace to account for the terrain and changing your position on the bike. You will also be developing your riding skills, something a turbo session will never do. So use the turbo when you have to, but whenever possible get outside and ride.

10
CROSS TRAINING

There will be times when it is not possible for you to get out and ride your bike or use an indoor trainer. The first option when you have time to train should always be to ride your bike, but if this is not possible then any endurance training will have some benefit in terms of improving your cardiovascular fitness.

If you are away on business, you may have to go to the hotel gym for a workout. If there is an exercise bike in there you can do your normal session, although it should be limited to a 60–90 minute endurance session or a shorter 20–30 minute threshold session. The gym bike will give you a decent workout, but try not to do it too often because your riding position will be different to the one you normally adopt on your road bike. You can try to adjust the saddle height to match your usual riding position, but it is always better to get on your road bike if you have the choice.

But what if there is no exercise bike either? What is the best form of cross training for an endurance cyclist? Well, any endurance exercise is better than none, so if you can run, swim or get on a rowing machine it's better than not training at all. Running is probably the best form of exercise for cyclists. Not only is it a great way to maintain cardiovascular fitness, but it works some of the same muscle groups as cycling (albeit in a different way). It's easy to do too as all you need is clothing to suit the climate and a pair of running shoes.

However, running does carry a higher risk of muscle and ligament injuries than cycling. This is because it's a weight-bearing exercise in which the runner's standing leg will endure a force equal to six times their body weight with each stride. Like any other activity, it takes time for your body to adapt. So if you have never done much running before, or not for a while, you need to ease yourself back into it.

If you'd rather not run but can get to the gym, then using a rowing machine is probably the next best thing. You could also try swimming. It's just a question of choosing the activity you prefer. If you are trying activities like running that are unfamiliar to you, it may be better just to do 10 minutes running, then 10 minutes on a rowing machine, followed by 10 minutes on a cross trainer, before finishing with 10 minutes on a stepper.

Rules of cross training

Cross training is not essential for the sportive rider, but if you do decide to use it when you can't ride here are the main guidelines. Stick to the principles of your cycling training programme. If you are in an endurance phase in the winter, any cross training you do should be aimed at improving endurance. Whether you opt for running, rowing or swimming, you should be doing steady efforts of around 20–30 minutes.

It is impossible to make a direct comparison between the benefits of cross training and endurance cycling. But as a general rule of thumb, if you should have been doing between one and two hours of endurance training on your bike, you would need to do between 40 and

60 minutes of running, or between 20 and 40 minutes on a rowing machine.

Running rules for cyclists

Start off gently running or jogging for 10 to 15 minutes in your first session before you become accustomed to it. If you have been in regular cycle training, you will have the cardiovascular endurance to cope with running, but your cycling muscles will not be used to the increased strain and stretching involved in running. You will find running easier if, during your cycle training programme, you have been doing regular stretching exercises. Because cyclists do not fully extend their leg when pedalling, their hamstrings tend to shorten. This can lead to problems if you try to run too fast too soon.

Make sure you get a good pair of running shoes with adequate cushioning that are appropriate for your running style. Some runners over-pronate or under-pronate – that is, their feet either flex too far inwards or outwards when landing on the ground. This may mean they need a particular type of shoe. If you are unsure, there are many specialist running shops that offer the use of a 'foot scan' device to determine the type of shoe you need.

Most running injuries are impact injuries, so wherever possible it's best to run on a soft surface to reduce the stress on your muscles and joints. Run on trails, park land or canal towpaths, rather than always running on the road. Once you have the right kit, and are happy that you can run for an extended period, you need to decide how long to run for and how fast.

Weight training

Many pro riders, such as Lance Armstrong, have included weight training as part of their winter programme. However, there remains controversy over the relevance of this type of training for endurance cyclists, and it is important to understand the theory behind the benefits before deciding whether to include weights in your own programme.

An elite endurance rider will have well-developed thigh muscles and may look immensely strong and powerful, but they are built for aerobic power production, not muscular power and strength. A track sprinter like Chris Hoy will need muscular strength and the ability to produce an all-out effort in a short period of time. For a sprinter, weight training can help develop the muscular strength needed for an all-out, maximal effort on the bike. In contrast, an endurance cyclist like Armstrong will need more extended aerobic power (measured in watts), maintained consistently over a longer period. They may need short bursts of speed and power, but these will be interspersed with long periods of endurance. For the endurance rider, it is therefore important to understand that the forces involved in turning the pedals are too low for muscular strength to be a key performance factor in endurance events.

Because the endurance or sportive rider needs aerobic power rather than muscular strength, the main improvements will come from developing your cardiovascular system. The benefits of weight training don't therefore have a direct influence on performance. Weight training has *no specific* carry-over to endurance cycling. However, cyclists can benefit from weight training because of its effect on body alignment and muscle balance.

In our analogy of the car, (Figure 7.2, page 65) the main determinant of performance is our engine: our aerobic or cardiovascular system. However, if the chassis of your car is bent, or the tracking is off, a lot of that power will be lost through inefficiency and eventually the car will break down. The same can be said about your body: poor alignment and muscle imbalances will prevent you from generating your power potential, and may even lead to injury and pain.

Muscle imbalances occur where the muscles around a joint or area of the body are not at their ideal length or tension. Some muscles acting on the joint will be weak, while others will be tight. A combination of stretching the tight and strengthening the weak muscles can correct the syndrome, bringing the joint into optimal alignment. When the muscles are balanced, the joint is able to maintain its optimal axis of rotation and has the potential to generate maximal force. Using weight training to correct muscle imbalances and poor alignment will not only enable you to get a better position on the bike, but also allow you to generate more power.

Indicators that suggest you might benefit from weight training are as follows:

- **Aches and pains** subsequent to training and not related to the prime movers for cycling (the legs and hips). A classic example would be lower back pain brought on by an increase in volume of training.
- **Poor climbing power, especially out of the saddle.** When climbing, the demands on your pelvis (or 'core') increase as your body uses it as a foundation for higher power production. The more power that needs to be generated, the more stable or solid the pelvis must be. Standing climbing in particular requires a functional, strong core to transmit power effectively between the upper and lower body.
- **Poor biomechanics/pedalling technique.** If you are finding it difficult to get a comfortable position on the bike, or to develop an efficient pedalling technique, lack of strength may be limiting your potential. If you notice you have an unusual pedalling style (such as erratic leg/knee movements, or knees or ankles rolling in or out), this may be an indicator of muscle imbalances that are limiting performance.
- **Poor muscle tone.** For novice riders who have come to the sport late, poor muscle tone may be an indication of poor general condition. Weight training can support an endurance programme by developing bigger and more numerous muscle fibres that can then be trained on the bike. This may particularly help with threshold and high-intensity training that requires adequate type 2a and 2b muscle fibre development.
- **Older riders** are more likely to need weight training to maintain good muscle tone due to the tendency of the muscles to atrophy (decrease in size) and weaken with age. The old adage 'if you don't use it you lose it' applies here and some older riders may benefit from overloading the muscles in the gym, because cycling on its own will not stimulate muscle development or maintenance.
- **Female riders** are also more likely to benefit from strength training because the wider female pelvis, and a tendency to have more endurance muscle fibres, can result in more alignment problems. Weight training can help maintain muscle balance and prevent injury that might otherwise occur because of these factors.

As with all aspects of your training programme, if you include weight training you should try to integrate it as part of your overall plan. Muscle soreness that can result from weight training will inhibit recovery between higher intensity, quality bike sessions. A well-planned programme will therefore ensure that, as the intensity of your cycling programme increases and your targeted event approaches, weight training will be limited or stopped all together. However, maintenance stretching and key corrective/balancing exercises that do not create soreness can help maintain your improved alignment and maximise your power-generating potential. These type of exercises can be included at any time during your training. Some key postural strength exercises will be included in the next section on stretching.

Seeking assistance with a weight training programme

If you decide that you would benefit from weight training, it is important to seek some assistance from an appropriately trained professional. Here is a rough guide as to which type of professional will be most appropriate:

- **Gym instructors.** If you have no real history of any pain or physical problems, your local gym instructor should be able to put you on the right road to making a start. Find an instructor who can show you how to safely perform some basic free weight exercises such as squats, dead lifts and bent-over rows, and ensure you always progress sensibly and lift with perfect form.
- **Personal trainers (PTs), strength conditioning specialists, CHEK exercise coaches (corrective exercise specialists).** If you are more committed to your weight training and would like a more advanced or personally tailored programme, then a PT or exercise specialist will be able to more closely meet your personal needs. Working alongside these people, you should have a written programme to follow that changes every six to eight weeks as your body adapts and changes.
- **CHEK practitioners, physiotherapists, other rehabilitation specialists.** If you have

an injury problem, or a history of injury, you should seek a specialist practitioner who has both training and experience in correcting muscle imbalances. These experts should carry out some kind of assessment first, including measures of muscle length/tension and strength, and provide a very precise programme including stretching/mobility for tight areas and strengthening exercises for weak areas.

TOP TIPS FOR FINDING A TRAINER

- **Trust your instincts.**
  A good exercise professional or rehab specialist will listen to what you want and make you feel confident that they are able to help. They will also make sure that your needs are met and that your programme is designed specifically for you.
- **Take up a referral.**
  If someone you know speaks highly of a specialist or has had good results with them, then try that specialist. Every profession has good and bad practitioners, so word of mouth is one of the best ways to help you get to the right person sooner.

Stretching

Like weight training, there is a lot of confusion about how and when to stretch, as well as which stretches are the most beneficial for cyclists. The approach we have taken here is to illustrate some key stretches that will help prevent tightness and stiffness in areas that tend to cause problems for cyclists. The exercises are designed to balance for the tightening that can occur due to the riding position, and also take into account the fact that many keen amateur cyclists have sedentary office jobs.

There are many reasons why you might stretch and each kind of stretching requires a different approach depending on its goal. In this book, the goal of the mobilisations and stretches is to broadly 'correct' and 'balance for' the effects of cycling and life in general. The exercises have been put together to be undertaken *after* a cycling training session, or in the evening before bed. If you have an injury history or known problem area, a more personal stretching programme should be sought from one of the above-mentioned professionals. However, this section should give the keen sportive rider a good idea of where to start.

Problems caused by stiffness and tightness

Muscle tightness and joint stiffness can be at least uncomfortable and at worst debilitating, as well as damaging to performance. When muscles become chronically short, they will produce discomfort on and off the bike, they may frequently cramp, and there will be an increased likelihood of an injury or tear. Joints that don't move will degenerate more quickly and there will be more stress and strain to the connective tissues around the area. By stretching muscles

that tend to get short, you can help them recover between bouts of cycling and prevent the progressive shortening that can lead to these problems.

The back

Immobility of the spine can be a significant problem for cyclists as they spend an unusual amount of time in a hunched-over position. This flexion (forward bend) can lead to stiffness or immobility in extension (bending backwards),

Figure 10.1 Flexion and extension

particularly since this is a movement people rarely need to perform. The problem is often exacerbated for the keen amateur who has a desk job and may be seated for most of the day in a flexed position, often with poor posture.

Where there is no counterbalancing mobility work, the body can, over time, begin to lose its ability to bend backwards. This excessive flexion can lead to a number of problems in both the upper and lower back (thoracic and lumbar spine). Muscles of the lower and upper back can become taut since they are constantly under strain, and this can cause discomfort and tension. The upper abdominal muscles under the ribs can also tighten due to being in a shortened position, further pulling the rib cage down and encouraging a slumped posture.

Continued flexion of the lower back or lumbar spine can lead to aggravation of the lumbar discs, which can begin to migrate or 'bulge' towards the spinal cord and nerves of the lower back. This can lead to a dull ache across the lower back and sometimes weakness or referred pain down one or both legs via the sciatic nerve (including 'sciatica').

Before stretching any muscles around this and other areas, it is important for the cyclist to develop and mobilise the joints and structures of the spine to counterbalance the static position held on the bike. A foam roller that is about 90 cm (3 ft) long, with a 10 cm diameter (4 inches), is a really helpful tool for mobilising the thoracic spine (upper back) into rotation and extension.

The longitudinal foam roller mobilisation

The longitudinal foam roller exercise not only mobilises the spine in rotation, but also has the benefit of stretching the ligament that runs along the front of the vertebrae. Because the roller moves it can also begin to stimulate some of the small stabiliser muscles in the lower back that can help to stabilise the joints.

Figure 10.2 Longitudinal foam roller mobilisation

- Start by lying on your back along the length of the roller. Make sure your head is on the roller, your knees are bent and your feet are flat on the floor.
- Cross your arms over your chest and take a few deep breaths in this position before you start to move. Try to breathe deeply into your tummy so that it rises on the in breath, and drops down on the out breath.

- Once you have got a relaxed breathing rhythm, drop your knees one way and your shoulders the other as you breathe out, so that you are twisting gently through the middle (as shown in Figure 10.2).
- Breathe in as you bring your shoulders and knees to the centre and, as you breathe out, drop your knees and shoulders the other way, twisting your body in the opposite direction.
- Repeat this movement 15–20 times, moving in time with your breathing.

If you find it difficult to balance on the roller to start with, rest your arms on the floor for extra balance. With practice, you will soon be able to progress to having only your elbows on the floor, and then your arms across your chest.

The horizontal foam roller mobilisation
It is a good idea to have practised the longitudinal foam roller exercise for a few weeks before starting on the horizontal one. Alternatively, you can check that your rib cage expands 4 cm (about 1.5 inches) with a deep inhalation before you use the foam roller in this way. This ensures that there is adequate movement to do the exercise safely.

To perform this test, run a tape measure around the bottom of your ribs, just below the sternum. (This would be roughly the level where you would put your heart rate monitor or as shown in Figure 10.3). Holding the tape measure lightly, take a deep breath and allow your rib cage to expand and stretch the tape under your fingers.

If you are able to expand your rib cage 4 cm further than your starting position, it is safe to go ahead with this exercise. If not, stick with the longitudinal exercise, work on your deep breathing, and keep retesting your rib expansion.

Figure 10.3 Rib expansion test

The horizontal foam roller mobilisation is designed to separate each segment or vertebrae of the spine in extension, so that they can move individually as they should, rather than getting 'stuck' and moving as chunks together. This exercise can be quite uncomfortable to start with and so you may have to ease yourself into it. If you find you cannot stand lying on the roller any more, roll off to the side rather than sitting up suddenly.

Figure 10.4 Horizontal foam roller mobilisation

- Start with the roller running across your body on the uppermost part of your back, but not your neck.
- Interlink your hands lightly behind your neck for support, being careful not to pull on your neck. Relax your head as much as possible.
- Take a deep breath into your stomach and, as you relax, let your body weight drop on to the roller as much as possible so that you arch backwards.

- Repeat on the same spot two or three times.
- Push with your legs to move your body up the roller. It should be positioned a few inches lower on your back.
- Once again, breathe into your stomach and, as you relax, let your body weight drop on to the roller.
- Repeat on the same spot two or three times before moving up the roller once again.
- Continue with this process until the roller is at the bottom of your thoracic spine, or opposite your lowest rib. Often this last spot is quite uncomfortable and can provoke shaking in the muscles!
- To finish the exercise, roll off to the side rather than sitting up.

The McKenzie press-up
The McKenzie press-up mobilises the lumbar spine (lower back) into extension (backward bending). This is a very important exercise for cyclists and anyone who spends any prolonged periods seated. It can help both to maintain mobility in this direction and to centralise the lumbar discs that can start to migrate backwards over time. This exercise can also be mildly uncomfortable to start with. As you progress through the exercise, any discomfort should ease and it should not last once you've finished. If you have pain or discomfort that doesn't ease throughout the exercise or afterwards, you should consult a physiotherapist or osteopath who will be able to help you further.

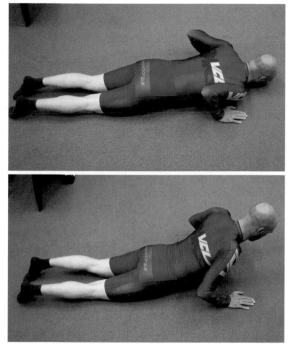

Figure 10.5 McKenzie press-up

- Start by lying on your front, with your hands positioned underneath your shoulders and your elbows tucked in.
- Take a deep breath and, as you breathe out, push yourself away from the floor, relaxing your hips and pelvis.
- Only go as high as you can while keeping your hips on the floor. Stop at the point at which you start to feel your pelvis lift up.
- Try to keep your hips, legs and back as relaxed as possible throughout this exercise.
- Breathe in as you lower yourself down to the floor, and breathe out as you push yourself up.

- Move in time with your breathing and repeat 10–20 times.
- As your mobility improves, you will find that you are able to lift your body higher before your hips start to come up off the floor.

The legs

Stretching your hamstrings at the knee

While the quadriceps at the front of the thigh are among the prime movers for cyclists, one of the worst problem areas for tightness is often the hamstrings at the back of the knee. This is because when cycling the knees rarely straighten completely. Only when the cyclist stands do the hamstrings at the back of the knee get a brief stretch and this is insufficient to have any influence on the length of the muscles. This is exacerbated in riders who spend a lot of time sat down at work, where the hamstrings at the back of the knee stay in a shortened position. Stretching the hamstrings is therefore very important for cyclists.

Many commonly performed hamstring stretches are combination stretches for the hamstrings at the knee, the hip and the lower back. While these can sometimes be helpful, cyclists need to be more specific in targeting the lower hamstrings at the knee. (The upper hamstrings and back are already stretched through being flexed forwards on the bike.) In practice, this means ensuring that the lower back stays extended or arched throughout the hamstring stretch. This technique can be difficult to start with and requires practice at maintaining a lumbar curve.

Figures 10.6 Hamstring stretches

- Start by lying on your back with both legs straight.
- Slide your hand underneath your lower back and create as much space as possible by gently arching your back. There should be just enough room for your hand to slide in and out of this gap.
- Bend one knee and grasp the leg at the back of the thigh, keeping the lower leg relaxed with your heel dropping down.
- To begin the stretch, straighten your leg slowly upwards. As you move, concentrate on maintaining the arch in your lower back.
- Only take your leg as high as it will go while you are maintaining the gap under your back. This ensures that the stretch is in the target area behind the knee.
- You can also gently pull your toes back towards your knee to increase the stretch.
- Hold this position for 20–30 seconds before relaxing out of the stretch, dropping your heel and relaxing your lower leg down.
- Repeat from three to six times on each leg, or until you feel that both sides are well matched. You may notice that you are tighter on one side than the other and it is important that you balance for this by stretching more on the tighter side.
- If it is too difficult to hold the position for 20 seconds to start with, hold for as long as you can and build up to 20–30 seconds.
- If you are very tight, you will find it hard to move at all while maintaining an arch. If this is the case, it can be useful to use a yoga strap or belt to hold your leg for longer periods. This is easier than having to use your thigh muscles to straighten your leg against a lot of tension (see Figure 10.6).
- As you improve the flexibility of your lower hamstrings, you should find that you are able to take your leg higher without changing the gap underneath your lower back.

The upper body
Although not among the prime movers in cycling, the upper body can get tight and tense

through resting the body weight on the handlebars. In particular, the chest and upper back can get short and tight, which can cause discomfort in these areas. It can also sometimes lead to injury to, or 'trigger points' in, the upper trapezius muscles of the upper back. 'Trigger points' are uncomfortable 'knots' in the muscle that can cause pain and often need to be ironed out with massage.

Stretching the pec minor and internal shoulder rotators

The pec minor is the small chest muscle at the front of the shoulder that can contribute to 'rounded shoulders' and poor posture in the upper body. In cyclists it often becomes tight in combination with the deep internal shoulder rotators, and stretching these can alleviate tension and reduce the risk of shoulder injury.

Figure 10.7 Pec minor stretches

- To stretch the pec minor, start by facing the wall and raise one arm so that your elbow is level with your shoulder, and at right angles.
- To stretch the internal shoulder rotators at the same time, turn your thumb backwards away from the wall.
- Placing your other hand in front of your other shoulder, gently push your body away from the wall, turning your head away and leaving the side that you are stretching (with the right-angled arm) as close to the wall as possible.
- As you do this, relax the shoulder on the side you are stretching as much as possible.
- As you push into the stretch position, you will feel mild discomfort at the front of the shoulder on the side with the right-angled arm.
- Hold this position for 20–30 seconds before relaxing out of the stretch by turning your body back to face the wall.
- Repeat three or four times on each side, or until you feel both sides are equally matched.

Stretching the upper trapezius and neck

In the cycling position, the upper trapezius (the 'coat hanger' shaped muscles at the top of the back) and the neck can carry a lot of tension. This is because your arms are extended forwards and your head tipped backwards. The stretch below can help alleviate these problems and prevent excessive tension building up in these areas.

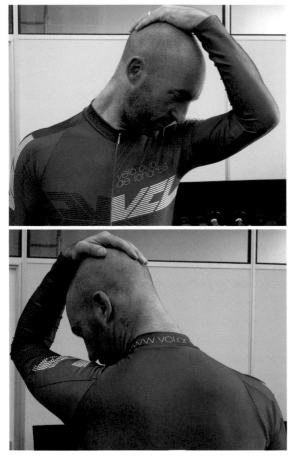

Figure 10.8 Upper trapezius and neck stretches

- Stand upright with good posture, picking your chest up and pulling your shoulders back.
- Turn your head to look left and then slide your hand over the top of your head, grasping it just below where you will feel your scull 'dips in'.
- Keeping your chin close to your chest, gently pull your head downwards and across, until you feel a mild stretch in the neck and upper back on the opposite side.

- As you pull gently into position, make sure the opposite shoulder stays down and doesn't hunch up towards your ear to avoid the stretch.
- Hold this position for 20–30 seconds before coming slowly out of the stretch and changing sides.
- Alternate between sides, repeating three or four times or until you feel both sides are even.

Summary

The table opposite summarises the stretching and mobilisation exercises described in this section. The whole routine will take you 16–27 minutes once you are practised in getting into and out of the positions. Here are some final tips on how to approach these exercises.

Stretching tips

- Try to perform the complete routine at least once or twice a week, ideally after your longest or most intense rides.
- This type of stretching is most effective when the body is warm, and so you may want to shower or bath when you get in from a ride before starting your stretching.
- If you train after work in the evening and have trouble 'winding down', stretching while you are watching television or listening to music can help shift the body into rest and recovery mode.
- *Don't* avoid or rush the stretches that you find the most difficult or uncomfortable. These are the ones that you need the most.

Table 10.1 Summary of exercises

Stretch/Mobilisation	Repetitions and instructions	Time taken
Longitudinal foam roller mobilisation	15–20 in time with your breathing	2–3 mins
Horizontal foam roller mobilisation	2–3 breaths on 6–8 sections of your back	1–2 mins
McKenzie press-ups	10–20 in time with your breathing	1–2 mins
Hamstrings at the knee	3–6 on each leg, or until you feel even, holding for 20–30 seconds	4–8 mins
Pec minor and internal shoulder rotators	3–4 each side, or until you feel even, holding for 20–30 seconds	4–6 mins
Upper trapezius and neck	3–4 each side, or until you feel even, holding for 20–30 seconds	4–6 mins

3

NUTRITION

11
GENERAL NUTRITION

While adequate and appropriate training may be the key to optimal race day performance, adequate and appropriate nutrition is the key to being able to train successfully.

Consider again the analogy of the Formula One car. To be able to complete the race distance, the car needs sufficient fuel. To be competitive in the race, the car needs to use the highest quality fuel in an optimal way. The fuel must be of a type to provide enough power for the duration of the race and to be used efficiently. If the car is powered by diesel instead of high-octane race fuel, the level of performance will be reduced.

As with the high performance car, the fuel required to power the endurance cyclist must be of the right type if that individual is to achieve their optimal performance. However, unlike a Formula One car, the human body has not one but three sources of energy: carbohydrate, fat and protein. In order to ensure optimal performance, these fuel sources must be consumed in the correct quantity and at the most appropriate time.

Basic dietary needs

Before considering what is important for the exercising individual, it is important to fully understand the basic nutritional requirements of the body. Good nutrition is essential to good health and prevention of disease. At rest, the requirement is to supply the body with sufficient nutrients for energy, building and repairing body tissue, and for maintenance of metabolic processes. In order to do this, we must provide our body with an adequate supply of macronutrients (carbohydrate, fat and protein); micronutrients (vitamins and minerals); and water.

Carbohydrate

Carbohydrate is the body's primary energy source because it is broken down more completely and efficiently than fat or protein. Its role is twofold: to provide energy for activity, and to provide a constant supply of blood glucose to enable functioning of the brain and the central nervous system. Because of this, the absolute minimum requirement of carbohydrate intake is 100 g per day, although the recommended minimum intake for the non-exercising adult is 130 g.

The secondary role of carbohydrate is to spare protein. When the carbohydrate supply is inadequate, protein is broken down into glucose. In this case, the key function of protein (growth and development of the body structures and tissue) is suppressed and it's used instead to ensure that the supply of blood glucose is maintained.

The final function of carbohydrate has to do with the metabolism of fat. Fat-burning occurs more completely and efficiently when sufficient carbohydrate is available. Without an adequate supply of carbohydrate, fat breakdown is incomplete, and the resultant ketones (fats that have not been broken down completely) will lead to fatigue, nausea, lack of appetite, and in extreme cases coma or even death.

The recommended target for carbohydrate intake is 55–60 per cent of calorific requirements for the normal individual. Additionally, to ensure health, no more than 25 per cent of daily calories should come from sugars.

Fat

Although considered by many as an unwelcome addition to the diet, fat has many key roles, and therefore must not be overlooked.

The primary function of fat is as a source of energy, secondary to the energy released from carbohydrate. Despite containing twice the energy of carbohydrate, fat isn't the preferred fuel of the body because it is slower and more difficult to metabolise. However, while the body cannot store large amounts of carbohydrate, fat stockpiled in adipose cells offers the largest and most efficient source of energy in the body, and therefore can provide almost limitless energy.

Additionally, fat has several other key roles including, most importantly, being a source of several key, fat-soluble vitamins and essential fatty acids, which cannot be manufactured by the body. Fat also helps to protect vital organs, acts as a source of insulation and is a lubricant for body tissue.

From a dietary perspective, fat adds moisture to food, making it more palatable and pleasant to consume. For this reason it is often easy to overindulge in high-fat foods. Ideally, the fat intake in your diet should provide between 20 and 35 per cent of the calories consumed, with less than 10 per cent of your total calories coming from saturated fats.

TIPS TO REDUCE DIETARY FAT INTAKE

- Reduce the use of butter and margarine on sandwiches or toast. Go without occasionally: it won't take long before you don't notice the difference.
- Consume lower-fat milk (while the difference between 2 and 4 per cent fat content seems small, it actually amounts to 20 g (0.7 oz) of fat in 1 litre (1.7 pints) of milk!).
- Use low-fat or fat-free salad dressing.
- Adopt low-fat cooking methods – avoid frying if possible, and grill, bake or steam your food instead.
- Choose tomato-based sauces or low-fat sauces rather than butter or cream-based sauces for pasta, rice or potatoes.
- Learn to read food labels! Processed and pre-packaged 'ready meals' can often have very high fat contents.

Protein

While carbohydrate and fat are the predominant energy sources in the body, the role of protein is slightly different. Although protein does have an energy yield that can be used to sustain one's metabolism should carbohydrate stores become depleted, it's mainly required for normal growth and development of the body structures and tissue.

Protein forms a part of every living cell, and differs from fat and carbohydrate in that it also contains nitrogen, in addition to carbon, oxygen and hydrogen. Protein itself is made of smaller organic compounds called amino acids. It has been suggested that the body contains over 50,000 different proteins, although only about 1,000 have been identified. Each specific protein is determined by the number, arrangement and variety of amino acids that it contains. Hence amino acids are often known as 'building blocks'.

Amino acids are classified as either essential or non-essential. The non-essential amino acids can be synthesised in the liver in sufficient quantities to maintain health. Essential amino acids, however, can't be manufactured by the body and must be acquired from dietary intake. All essential amino acids must be available in sufficient quantities at all times to ensure adequate synthesis of vital proteins. If you don't have enough, health problems will develop.

Dietary proteins are classified as complete proteins (for example, meat, milk, cheese and eggs) when they contain enough of all the essential amino acids to maintain tissue and support growth. Incomplete proteins (such as bread, pulses and nuts) lack one or more of the essential amino acids. This does not mean that these foods should be avoided, because a mixture of incomplete proteins will combine to meet the bodily requirements. Generally speaking, complete proteins derive from animal sources, and incomplete proteins come from plant-based foods. Eating a variety of foods is recommended in order to ensure that all the amino acids are obtained.

The specific function of the individual protein is dependent on its composition in terms of amino acids. However, proteins have several major functions in the body. Primarily, they are vital for maintenance, growth and repair of body tissue. They are also crucial in the regulation of body processes, being essential in the manufacture of hormones and enzymes. They function within the immune system, creating specific antibodies giving protection from infection and disease, as well as assisting in blood-clotting. Plasma proteins function in the regulation of body fluid and electrolyte balance. Finally, and as we've mentioned above, if carbohydrate or fat levels are inadequate, proteins can be used as an energy source.

To meet the basic needs of health, the recommended daily allowance of protein is 0.8 g for each kilogram of the individual's body weight, and it should provide a minimum of 10 per cent of the daily energy intake. While this may be appropriate for the non-exercising person, the needs of the exercising individual will be reviewed later.

Micronutrients

The term micronutrient, which is commonly used to describe vitamins and minerals, refers to the fact that these substances are needed in very small quantities. Nevertheless, although neither is a source of energy, vitamins and minerals are a crucial part of the diet.

Vitamins

The key role of vitamins is to facilitate the chemical reactions in the body associated with normal metabolism, growth and development. Each vitamin has a very specific function that cannot be substituted by other compounds. Because vitamins cannot be manufactured by the body, appropriate intake is crucial to well-being. When vitamin intake is inadequate, this will not only impact on normal bodily function, but can also result in longer term health issues.

Vitamins are classified as either water soluble or fat soluble. Termed 'water soluble' since they are found in the watery portion of food, this group of vitamins is absorbed directly into the bloodstream. Since they are held in solution, they are not stored and therefore need to be consumed daily. Vitamin C and the B complex vitamins are water-soluble vitamins. When consumed in excess, this classification of vitamins is excreted in urine, although too much can be toxic.

Vitamins classified as fat soluble are, as the name suggests, absorbed with fats, and can be stored in the liver or the adipose (fat) tissue within the body. Because of the ability of the body to store these vitamins, daily intake is not required. Fat-soluble vitamins are A, D, E and K. Excess intake of these vitamins, particularly A and D, can have serious consequences, including liver or kidney damage.

The guidelines set by nutrition experts for recommended daily allowance (RDA) of vitamins are sufficient for both the 'normal' and athletic population. Furthermore, despite heavy marketing from supplementation companies, vitamins are found in all major food groups, and therefore intake from a healthy and varied diet should be sufficient to meet the individual's needs. Where an individual does not have an additional, medically defined need for vitamins and yet still desires to use supplements, these should be consumed at a level no greater than the RDA.

Minerals
Minerals are inorganic substances that are required for promoting growth and maintaining health. Unlike vitamins, they become part of the body structure, making up approximately 4 per cent of total body weight, and are found in all tissues and body fluids.

Minerals are essential to diet because they have two key functions. The first is providing structural support, by giving strength to bones, teeth, skin, hair and nails. The second is a regulatory function: specific minerals are involved with maintaining fluid balance, nerve cell transmission, and muscle contraction.

Minerals are found in all major food groups, however either excessive or insufficient mineral intake can cause health problems. Calcium and sodium intakes currently appear to cause the biggest problem in the western world. As with all the other nutrients, a healthy and varied diet will provide the appropriate intake and supplementary sources should not be required.

Water balance

The final consideration in our discussion of general dietary requirements is water. Because water constitutes around 60–65 per cent of total body weight in the adult male, and approximately 50–55 per cent of body weight in the adult female, ensuring adequate hydration is one of the most basic nutritional requirements. Yet it is often overlooked.

Water is lost in several ways. Fluid is lost through sweat, during both warm weather and exercise; and also through excretion. Insensible water loss also occurs, mostly through the breath, but also through the skin. It is easy to become moderately dehydrated over a number of days. Without water intake, a person can survive for no longer than a week; without food they can survive a month!

Water is essential because it has many functions. Water:

- gives shape to cells;
- helps form the structure of large molecules, such as glycogen and protein;
- serves as a lubricant in mucus secretions and joint fluid;
- has a transport function in the body, both taking nutrients to the cells, and clearing waste products from them;
- aids in the regulation of body temperature;
- is a medium for chemical reactions.

PROMOTING FLUID INTAKE

- Drink before you get thirsty!
- Carry a bottle of water with you, and make a note of how many times it is refilled.
- Drink beverages you enjoy.
- Drink a glass of water with each meal.
- Eat plenty of fruit and vegetables with a high water content.
- Curb your consumption of beverages that contain diuretic properties, such as caffeine.

Dehydration will not only affect your level of sports performance, but in the non-exercising state can leave you with a general sense of fatigue, headaches, a loss of appetite, or even feeling light-headed and nauseous.

On average, total daily fluid loss is approximately 2.6 litres (4.5 pints). In order to maintain fluid balance, fluid intake should therefore meet this output. For a non-exercising individual, it is recommended that a minimum of approximately 2 litres (3.5 pints) of fluid should be consumed per day, increasing in warm weather and during exercise. The additional fluid required to maintain fluid balance will come from food and one's metabolism.

HOW HYDRATED ARE YOU?

Clinically, hydration state is measured by assessing urinary specific gravity or urine osmolality. This is a simple test to see how many solutes your urine contains – essentially the concentration of your urine.

At home, the easiest assessment is to take the 'pee test'. The first part of the urine stream is discarded, then ideally a small sample of urine is collected in a clear container. This should then be compared to a colour chart (Armstrong, L.E. (2000), Performing in Extreme Environments, Human Kinetics. Champaign, IL.). In simple terms, however, the darker the urine, the more dehydrated you are. A clear, or lightly coloured, sample is what you are hoping to produce. If not, you may need to review the amount of fluid you are consuming. Ideally you should take this test first thing in the morning. However, you can also review and assess hydration status as a result of training.

Note, however, that certain medicines and vitamins may cause the urine colour to change, and if any of these have been taken, the test may be unreliable.

Resting dietary composition

Once you know where the energy should come from, the key is to get the proportions correct. Scientific data has suggested that the resting energy requirements are approximately 42 per cent from carbohydrate, 41 per cent from fat and 17 per cent from protein. Therefore, if energy is consumed in these ratios and in appropriate quantities, it is sufficient to maintain both health and a constant body weight for sedentary individuals.

Although these values differ from those proposed above, they closely match the composition of the typical western diet for both athletes and non-athletes alike (Blair et al., 1981). However, getting the balance of nutrients correct is only a small part of what's required. An issue of far greater importance is the correct calculation of required energy intake. Getting it wrong accounts for the rise in body fat percentage in sedentary individuals and the general increase in levels of obesity.

Thus far, only the needs for general nutrition have been considered. When we look at the requirements of the endurance athlete (see Chapters 14 and 15), the balance of energy sources will change.

Normal 'healthy' diet

While we are sure many readers would love to be presented with a dietary plan to meet their 'ideal' needs for balance of nutrients and correct energy intakes, the key to achieving a 'healthy' and 'balanced' diet is variety.

The concept that some foods are 'bad' for you, while others are 'good', oversimplifies the complex interaction of foodstuffs. Essentially, nutrients do not exist in isolation, and therefore are not eaten individually.

The key is to enjoy a wide variety of foods, both in each meal and in your general diet. The widely available food pyramid (Figure 11.1) thus acts as a good model for food use and variety, allowing you to choose plenty of what is good for you, but still enjoying a little of what may be considered less beneficial.

Figure 11.1: An example of the food pyramid

Most of your diet, as you will no doubt already be aware, should be made up of complex carbohydrates such as bread, cereals, rice, pasta and potatoes. Fresh fruit and vegetables will then not only provide additional sources of carbohydrate, but will also ensure you get essential vitamins and minerals.

Essential fats should preferably come from dairy produce such as milk, eggs or yoghurt. Additional fats and also protein will be obtained from fish, white meat and beans or nuts.

Reference
(Blair, S., Ellsworth, M., Haskell, W., Stern, M., Farquhar, J. & Wood, P. (1981) 'Comparison of nutrient intake in middle-aged men and women runners and controls.' *Medicine and Science in Sports and Exercise*, 13: 310–15).

12
FUEL FOR SPORT

Having examined the dietary requirements for health and well-being, it is important to understand how these requirements may change for individuals involved with physical activity. A typical adult male of 80 kg (12 st 8 lb) and 15 per cent body fat will have the capacity to store carbohydrate in muscle to a maximum of 300–400 g (10.5–14 oz), and a total liver store of 80–100 g (3–3.5 oz). This means that, when the body is fully loaded with carbohydrate, at best it will have available 500 g (17.6 oz). With each 1 g (0.03 oz) of carbohydrate yielding just over 5 kcal of energy, the total energy available from carbohydrate is approximately 2,000 kcal.

In comparison, the same individual will be carrying a total of 12 kg (26 lb) of fat, which equates to over 50 times the amount of energy stored within carbohydrate (approximately 115,000 kcal). If that individual should lose a large proportion of their fat mass, and be carrying just 6 per cent body fat (the equivalent of an elite endurance athlete), their total body mass would fall to 72.3 kg (159 lb). With a drop of 7.7 kg (17 lb) of body fat, they would still be storing around 40,000 kcal of energy as fat. This fat store would increase by 10.7 kg (23.5 lb) and a total of around 215,000 kcal for someone carrying 25 per cent body fat (Table 12.1).

Table 12.1 Percentage body fat, fat mass, and energy available

Weight	% Body fat	Lean mass	Fat mass	Approximate fat energy (kcal)
72.3 kg (159 lb)	6	68.0 kg (150 lb)	4.3 kg (9.5 lb)	40,000
80.0 kg (176 lb)	15	68.0 (150 lb)	12.0 kg (26.4 lb)	115,000
90.7 kg (200 lb)	25	68.0 (150 lb)	22.7 kg (50 lb)	215,000

Energy efficiency

So with all this energy available from fat, why are the limited stores of carbohydrate of importance? Quite simply, the burning of fat as a fuel is a long slow process, and does not yield as high an energy release as carbohydrate. Oxygen is needed to burn either fat or carbohydrate, but unfortunately there is a limit to how much oxygen the body can take up and use. For an elite endurance athlete, this can be as much as 5–7 litres every minute. But for a typical sportive rider, the maximal oxygen consumption is more likely to be around 4 litres per minute, with the individual being able to sustain about 75 per cent of maximal capacity (about 3 litres per minute).

For each litre of oxygen consumed, the energy yield from fat is 4.686 kcal, and from carbohydrate it is 5.047, This means that during high-intensity work, where the ability to consume oxygen is near its limit, the body will preferentially burn carbohydrate because it provides a greater amount of energy. The final twist to the release of energy is that, for each litre of oxygen used, approximately 0.5 g (0.02 oz) of fat is burned, whereas nearly 1.25 g (0.04 oz) of carbohydrate is utilised.

So for every minute of exercise, the well-trained individual consuming 4 litres of oxygen would be burning 5 g (0.18 oz) of carbohydrate. This means that a full carbohydrate store is only enough to sustain 100 minutes of exercise before the energy source is depleted, and exercise has to slow or stop completely. This is the process that occurs when the sportive rider 'bonks' or gets 'hunger knock'. Both muscle and blood levels of carbohydrate are at such a low level that exercise cannot be continued. (In some very extreme cases, full brain function cannot be sustained, and collapse occurs.)

This feeling of exhaustion is caused because, although the body can utilise fat stores to keep you going, it can only supply a much smaller amount of energy from fat than it can from carbohydrate. This is an extreme situation, and what happens before the body reaches this point is that fat is burned when exercising at a low intensity, with carbohydrate being used when the intensity increases.

So if you were riding at 15 km/h (around 10 mph) on a flat route, it would be possible for even a moderately fit rider to cycle along burning fat alone. But if that same rider cycles hard for 40 minutes with a series of flat-out sprint efforts, it would be possible for them to completely exhaust their carbohydrate store.

How much fat and carbohydrate you can utilise is dependent on the efficiency of your cardiovascular system – that is, how efficient you are in getting oxygen to the muscle. The more oxygen you can get to the muscle per minute, the more able your body is to use fat as a fuel source before needing to dig into its carbohydrate reserves. In a long-distance sportive ride this is obviously a crucial factor. You want to be able to ride as far as possible in fat-burning mode, saving your precious carbohydrate stores for the latter part of the race.

The effect of diet

Despite the fact that exercise intensity and oxygen uptake have a major effect on the ability to sustain endurance exercise, it is not the only key factor in your ability to keep going for a longer ride. The level of dietary carbohydrate has a significant impact on the levels of muscle glycogen (the storage form of carbohydrate). In 1967 Bergstrom and his colleagues (Bergstrom et al., 1967) clearly demonstrated the effects of a low (5%), moderate (40%) and high (82%) carbohydrate diet (as Figure 12.1 demonstrates). When individuals eat the low carbohydrate diet, glycogen levels remained low, and the athletes could only tolerate moderate-intensity exercise for 60 minutes before fatigue. With high carbohydrate intake, muscle glycogen storage was high, and athletes exercised for over three hours before fatigue. This is one of many examples showing the importance of high dietary carbohydrate for individuals undertaking exercise.

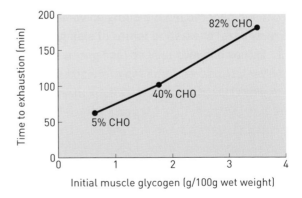

Figure 12.1 The effect of high, moderate and low carbohydrate diets on the ability to undertake endurance exercise. Bergstrom et al 1967, Acta Physiologica Scandinavica, Wiley-Blackwell Publishing.

Repeated days training

In 1980, Costill and Miller published scientific data that suggested that, when individuals consuming a moderate carbohydrate intake (with carbohydrate supplying 45–50% of the daily energy requirements) undertook just an hour of moderate to intense exercise every day, it took only three days to empty a moderately full glycogen store. If a high carbohydrate diet (65–70% of daily dietary requirements) was consumed, the result was near full repletion of the glycogen stores, allowing normal training on subsequent days (see Figure 12.2). More recently, work at Sportstest has shown that a high carbohydrate intake enables competitive performance to be maintained in three days of simulated competition, whereas large drops in performance occurred when only a moderate carbohydrate diet was consumed.

Thus, the overwhelming wealth of scientific data suggests that to maintain optimal performance,

sufficient levels of dietary carbohydrate need to be consumed. Around 60–75 per cent of daily energy intake should come from carbohydrates. This will ensure that carbohydrate burned during exercise is replaced daily. In order to compensate for differing body sizes, the intakes can be related to body mass. Target intake will be between 5 and 10 g of carbohydrate per kg of body mass. The actual quantity needed will be determined by the amount of exercise being undertaken (in terms of hours per day), the intensity of exercise (the higher the intensity, the more carbohydrates are burned), and also the type of exercise (weight-bearing exercise, such as running, requires a greater amount of energy than non-weight-bearing exercise, such as swimming or cycling).

Protein burning

As we've mentioned, in addition to its main job of providing energy for activity, carbohydrate has a protein-sparing role. This is particularly

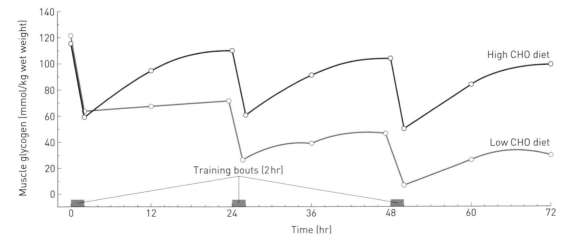

Figure 12.2 The impact of high and low carbohydrate diets on muscle glycogen levels during repeated days exercise. Costill & Miller 1980, IJSM

evident during training. Data from the early 1980s shows that protein breakdown significantly increases as a result of exercise. This is not surprising, because part of the purpose of training is to stimulate increased growth of muscle fibre by causing minor breakdown. However, the most interesting factor from this research is that more than twice as much protein is broken down when dietary, and therefore muscular, carbohydrate levels are low than when they are high. This is clearly illustrated in Figure 12.3, and it re-emphasises the need for a high carbohydrate diet and adequate protein intakes while training.

The importance of hydration

In addition to energy requirements, maintaining hydration at rest and during exercise is vital to the performance of the body. One of the first things to happen when you start exercising is that your body temperature rises and you begin to sweat. Even in the depths of winter you will be sweating to dissipate heat and keep your body temperature down. Individuals can lose more than 3 litres (5 pints) of fluid per hour when exercising in hot conditions. The fluid you lose reduces the blood volume, which places greater strain on your cardio-vascular system, increasing your heart rate and reducing the efficiency of oxygen delivery.

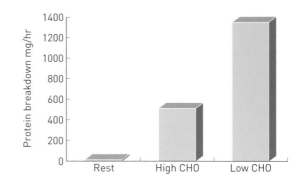

Figure 12.3 Effect of carbohydrate levels on protein breakdown, adapted from Lemon and Nagel.: Medicine and Science in Sport and Exercise 13(3), (1981)

Sweating increases with exercise intensity, so the harder you are working the more fluid you need to drink. Riders with a higher percentage of body fat will find it more difficult to dissipate heat and so will sweat more. Smaller, lean riders will generally find it easier to cope with excessive heat than larger riders because they will have a larger skin surface when compared to their body mass and so will be able to dissipate heat more quickly.

A decrease in body weight of between one and two per cent due to sweat loss will result in performance being reduced by up to 20 per cent. So you can see how important it is for the endurance athlete to be aware of the problems that come with dehydration.

References

Bergstrom, J., Hermansen, L., Hultman, E. & Saltin, B. (1967) 'Diet, muscle glycogen and physical performance.' *Acta Physiologica Scandinavica*, 71: 140–50. Wiley-Blackwell Publishing.

Costill, DL & Miller, JM (1980) 'Nutrition for endurance sport: carbohydrate and fluid balance.' *International Journal of Sports Medicine*, 1: 2–14. Georg Thieme Verlag.

Lemon, PWR and Nagel, FJ (1981) 'Effects of exercise on protein and amino acid metabolism.' *Medicine and Science in Sport and Exercise* (13(3): 141–149. Lippincott Williams & Wilkins Inc.

13
OPTIMAL NUTRITION FOR EXERCISE

Having provided some insight into the changes in metabolism and fuel utilisation from rest to exercise, and into the resulting impact on the body's ability to perform endurance exercise, in this section we will look at nutritional strategies before, during and after training to achieve optimal exercise. We will begin with the role nutrition plays in recovering from a training session. This may seem a back-to-front way of looking at it, but there is a valid reason for approaching it this way.

Recovery is the key to optimising the benefits you get from training. Training is simply the stimulus the body requires to initiate its adaptation to cope with increasing physical demands made upon it. Changes in muscle tissue, in the cardiovascular system and in the

efficiency of your metabolism occur as a response to training (that's to say, in the recovery phase) and not during the training itself. Get your recovery right and you will be able to train harder and more frequently, which will mean more rapid improvements in fitness. Get your recovery wrong, and you will soon find yourself fatigued!

Nutrition for recovery
Timing
As we emphasised earlier, during exercise carbohydrates are the predominant fuel used by the body. Consider an example of a rider using 180 g of carbohydrate per hour during a steady endurance effort. If they've done a one-hour ride, and taken carbohydrate drinks or gels during that ride, they will only have

been able to replace around 60 g of carbohydrate. After just 60 minutes of riding, they will already have a deficit of around 120 g of carbohydrate.

Intake of carbohydrate before exercise may top up liver glycogen and blood glucose to ensure the best possible start to the ride; and intake of carbohydrates during exercise will prolong exercise. But, as we will show, this will not be sufficient to meet all the demands of exercise. Therefore, following even a short training session such as the one mentioned in the previous paragraph, there will be a need to restore glycogen. This emphasises the importance of an appropriate recovery strategy.

Due to an increase in enzyme activity following exercise, there is a window of around two hours in which the body is better able to replenish its carbohydrate stores. So it is critical to start the recovery process as soon as possible after a training session, ideally within 10 or 15 minutes of the session ending.

Carbohydrate
The current scientifically based guidelines from the International Olympic Committee (2003) suggest that endurance athletes should aim to consume 1 g of carbohydrate per kilogram of body weight after training (approximately 50–100 g of carbohydrate dependent on body weight). This intake can be repeated hourly, possibly at frequent intervals, until the normal meal pattern is resumed. This is appropriate for a typical

endurance ride of between 90 minutes and two hours, but the strategy may need to be refined to take account of individual needs or different training sessions.

Protein
In addition to carbohydrate, it may also be important to take on board some protein. Around 15–20 g (0.5–0.7 oz) of protein combined with the recommended amount of carbohydrate may improve the rate at which muscle glycogen stores can be replaced. It is also available to help repair any muscle tissue damaged during exercise.

Rehydration
Along with restoring your energy needs, you also need to make sure you replace water lost during exercise. You need to drink between 1.2 and 1.5 litres (2.1–2.6 pints) of fluid for each kilogram of weight lost. Therefore, if you have lost 1 kilogram (2.2 lb) of weight during your ride, this equates to 1 litre (1.7 pints) of fluid (sweat) loss, and you need to drink around 1.25 litres (2.2 pints). If your body weight is down by 2 kilograms (4.4 lb), you need to drink around 2.5–3 litres (4.3 pints). Of course, this fluid should be taken in gradually at a comfortable rate. Once your body weight is back to normal you can return to drinking fluid normally.

In addition to replacement of fluid, replenishment of salts lost through sweating may also be required. Foods can usually replace all the salt needed, but some individuals find it difficult or impractical to eat immediately following exercise. In this case, beverages containing electrolytes can be beneficial. Not only will the electrolyte content aid fluid uptake, but the addition of sodium and potassium in a drink will often increase its palatability, thereby encouraging the athlete to drink post exercise.

Sports recovery drinks

While you can consume solid food and drink water, the easiest and most effective way of maximising your recovery is to use a sports recovery drink immediately following exercise, and then begin to eat normally within one or two hours post exercise. There are many such drinks on the market, but it is important to use one of the products that is palatable and easy to transport to your training or competition venue. Powder forms that mix with water are usually ideal. There are some recovery drinks that are mixed with milk, but the addition of milk may slow down the rate at which the nutrients can be absorbed and so delay the recovery process. Care may also be needed when using milk-based products in terms of total dietary fat intake.

Figure 13.1 Recovery time

Eating solid food is fine if no sports recovery drink is available, but it may not be the preferred option because it can take several hours to digest solid food. For example, an unripe (green-yellow skin) banana will take from four to six hours to be fully digested and its carbohydrate absorbed. If carbohydrate-rich foods are to be consumed, those with a moderate to high glycaemic index (GI) are preferred. Bread, fruit juices, sugar, jam, honey, and breakfast cereals should all be adequate.

For individuals looking to exercise twice per day, a specifically formulated recovery drink is always the preferred option because it is the quickest way to supply your body with all the energy it needs. If you are expecting to have 24 hours or more recovery between training sessions, these issues are not as critical. In either case, the immediate post-exercise recovery should be followed, around two or three hours after training has been completed, by a normal meal.

EATING FOR RECOVERY: KEY POINTS

- Eat approximately 1.0 g (0.04 oz) of carbohydrate per body weight (that is, about 50–100 g) within 15 minutes of training.
- 15–20 g (0.5–0.7 oz) protein can assist in improving recovery rate.
- Rehydrate at a comfortable rate to replace all sweat loss.

Nutrition prior to training

This is one the most contentious areas of sports nutrition research. Ideally, if appropriate and adequate recovery nutrition has been applied, and the athlete has taken sufficient care over 'resting' nutrition, pre-exercise nutrition should serve only to 'top up the tank'. However, studies of pre-exercise nutrition strategies have investigated different regimes where starting levels of muscle glycogen vary widely. There may also be significant variation in responses to different strategies between individuals. This makes the provision of a scientifically determined 'optimal' strategy nearly impossible.

For endurance training, as we have already seen, it is vital to ensure the carbohydrate stores in the body are as replete as possible. The period prior to exercise is therefore critical to maximise and/or top up glycogen stores.

Pre-exercise carbohydrate intake

The current advice on preparation for endurance competition from the Medical Commission of the International Olympic Committee is to consume 1–4 g (0.04–0.14 oz) of carbohydrate per kilogram of body weight in the six-hour period prior to exercise. Alternatively, they suggest that when a carbohydrate load strategy (see below) has been employed, the athlete should consume no carbohydrate in the six hours pre-exercise.

So the recommendations encompass a massive range – from zero to 320 g (11 oz) for an 80 kg

(176 lb) individual. The best advice that can realistically be given is to try a variety of strategies and find what works best for you in that particular competitive situation.

Three to four hours pre-training
In order to maximise your carbohydrate stores, you should have a high carbohydrate meal three or four hours prior to training. That allows the body time to digest the majority of the food and clear the system before training commences.

Two hours pre-training
If it is not possible to eat three or four hours pre-exercise, or if it feels appropriate to curb hunger, around two hours before exercise may be a good time to have a light carbohydrate snack containing about 50–80 g (1.8–2.8 oz) of carbohydrate.

In practice, if you are training or racing first thing in the morning, neither of these options may be possible. It's probably not advisable to lose a couple of hours sleep in order to have a pre-training meal. In this case, nutritional intake from solid food may be best avoided, or possibly substituted with an energy replacement drink.

Within two hours of training
After this time, the research is equivocal as to further carbohydrate intake. Where muscle glycogen levels are not replete, further consumption of carbohydrate does not appear to have a marked impact on subsequent exercise

metabolism. However, where carbohydrate stores are not completely full, intake of carbohydrate in the 30 to 60 minutes prior to exercise may elevate blood glucose and insulin. This results in an elevation of carbohydrate metabolism, and suppression of fat metabolism, during the first 30 minutes of exercise. In turn, this could potentially reduce the time taken to exhaust the carbohydrate stores, and ultimately cause fatigue.

A further consequence of consuming solid food within the final two hours prior to exercise is the potential gastric discomfort that could be caused if the food has not been fully digested or absorbed. It is therefore suggested that food is either avoided during this time, or at least that the athlete experiments to find a strategy that best fits their individual needs.

Early morning exercise
The practicalities discussed thus far suggest that, while it may be possible to consume solid food prior to early morning exercise, it may be better to have a good, high-carbohydrate meal the night before. If adequate time is available between waking and exercise, it may be possible to consume 50–80 grams (1.8–2.8 oz) of carbohydrate. If this is not practical, then exercise can be begun without prior nutrition.

Pre-exercise fluid ingestion
In addition to carbohydrate requirements, the need for pre-exercise hydration should not be overlooked. If you are eating solid food two hours before training, it is advisable to also

have around 400–700 ml (14–24 fl oz) of fluid at the same time. This will mean you are properly hydrated before the ride, and yet allow time for urination of excess fluid. Some athletes actually find it beneficial to avoid solid food intake at this time, and prefer to combine the required fluid and carbohydrate loads within a sports drink.

The final 15 minutes

For training sessions of longer than one hour, or where sweat loss may be heavy (for example, on an indoor trainer) the final 10–15 minutes before you start your ride (or warm-up for a competition) can be used to provide a final top-up of fluid and fuel to the body.

Around 200–600 ml (6–20 fl oz) of fluid can be sipped gradually over this time. It should leave you feeling 'comfortably full', but not bloated. This intake of fluid will fill the stomach. Sports science research tells us that maintaining a steady flow of fluid to the stomach during exercise, and keeping it slightly stretched, will promote emptying to the intestine and thereby fluid absorption. Hence the pre-exercise intake is the first stage in priming the body to better accept fluid, and maintain hydration status. In the same way that a water tank in a house is constantly topped up when water is used for a shower, the body works better when the supply of water to the stomach is topped up too.

If you are consuming pre-exercise fluids, topping up your energy levels immediately prior to exercising is also wise. The inclusion of 20–40 g (0.7–1.4 oz) of carbohydrate means that, by the time your training session begins, this energy will just be reaching the blood and will be ready for use, though without creating an insulin response in the body that could cause a dip in energy levels.

Going out on a training ride with a stomach comfortably full of fluid can take some getting used to if you haven't tried this method before. But it's worth persevering with this, because it allows you to have the maximum amount of energy available for your training session. It will also pay dividends on race day.

PRE-EXERCISE NUTRITION: KEY POINTS

- Three-four hours before: normal meal, containing 50–200 g (1.8–7 oz) of carbohydrate.
- Approximately two hours before: light snack containing 50–80 g (1.8–2.8 oz) carbohydrate, if required.
- Between 30 minutes and two hours before: possibly avoid solid food intake.
- Immediately prior to exercise (10–15 minutes pre warm-up): 200–400 ml (6–14 fl oz) of a 5–10 per cent (20–40 g) carbohydrate drink.

Nutrition during training

As we have seen previously, carbohydrate is the predominant fuel used during any form of exercise, and in particular it plays a key role in optimising performance during endurance exercise. So, when training, it is carbohydrate that must be replaced to enable the athlete to complete the training session effectively, and to make sure they recover as quickly as possible before the next training ride.

Carbohydrate uptake

Despite carbohydrate oxidation rates in excess of 2–3 g per minute, even with low-intensity exercise, during a training ride your body can only process ingested energy at a rate of about 1 g of carbohydrate per minute. That is, it is only possible to get a maximum of about 1 g of carbohydrate per minute from ingested drinks or gels to the working muscle.

As a general rule, it is advisable to scale this intake to match your body size and take in 1 g per kilogram of body weight for every hour of the training. For example, an 80 kg (176 lb) rider would consume approximately 80 g (2.8 oz) of carbohydrate per hour. In order to provide a constant source of energy, this means consuming carbohydrate on a regular basis, perhaps sipping a carbohydrate drink every 5–10 minutes – not waiting until 30 minutes into your ride and gulping down half a bottle of energy drink! Little and often is the key.

Solid or liquid?

On longer training sessions, or during events, many riders prefer to consume solid food to deliver their energy requirements. Scientific evidence suggests that the energy yield from solids can be as beneficial as from gels or fluids. However, the key choice that the individual should make when deciding the most appropriate strategy is whether the energy form will empty from the stomach rapidly, and if it is likely to cause any gastro-intestinal disturbances such as discomfort, bloating, or even vomiting or diarrhoea.

Solid foods will often take longer to empty from the stomach than fluids, particularly as they may also contain fat and dietary fibre. This can in turn increase the possibility of stomach upset, or suppress required fluid consumption due to a 'full' feeling. However, solid foods may be more portable and very concentrated, and they can often be of benefit when a long day in the saddle is planned by alleviating a hungry or empty feeling.

As with many of the nutritional practices, the key is to determine a strategy that works for you for a variety of exercise intensities, durations and climatic conditions.

Training of less than an hour

For a training session of less than one hour, some carbohydrate intake may be beneficial. It is unlikely that you will exhaust your carbohydrate store in under an hour unless you undertake a really hard interval session. On the other hand, we have to constantly be aware of the strategy of training and recovery.

If you feed during a training session that lasts one hour or less, you will have started to replenish the carbohydrate that you are burning. While it is unlikely that you will finish the training session in an 'energy neutral' situation – that is to say, you have virtually the same amount of carbohydrate stored in the body at the end of training as you did at the beginning – the amount of glycogen that will need to be replenished will be less. This means you should recover faster for the next session.

Fluid needs

As we have already shown, sweat loss during exercise can vary widely due to environmental conditions and exercise intensity. In order to avoid the adverse effects of dehydration, it is vital to replenish as much of the fluid loss as practical. Scientific evidence suggests that while cycling it may be possible to absorb as much as 1.4 to 1.6 litres (2.5 – 2.8 pints) of fluid per hour. However, this figure is reduced as exercise intensity increases. Ideally, it is best to finish a

HOW MUCH TO DRINK

It may be important to assess how much you sweat, in order to calculate how much to drink, for both winter and summer training.
Here's the easy way:

- Jump on the scales (preferably naked) before you train, remembering to keep a note of your weight. Don't forget to get dressed before you go training or you may get arrested!
- Enjoy your session, and drink as you normally would. Recording your fluid intake (mentally or otherwise) can also be of use to help calculate your sweat rate.
- Weigh yourself as soon after the training session as possible (naked and towelled dry).
- Any difference in body mass is sweat loss that you have not replaced. Every 0.5 kg (1.1 lb) lost equals 500 ml (16 fl oz) fluid! (You may be surprised how much you sweat, even in winter.)
- Add the body mass lost to volume consumed: this equals total sweat loss. To calculate sweat rate, divide the total amount by the time spent training. This will give you an idea of the fluid needed for the intensity, duration and weather conditions of future sessions.
- Finally, the chances are you that have not fully hydrated during your training session. So in order to fully rehydrate, drink 1.25 times the volume of weight lost.

ride with minimal dehydration, to maintain optimal performance.

During training and racing, fluid intake should be prioritised, and drinking should start soon after the training session commences. The key to maintaining hydration status is then to keep drinking small amounts on a regular basis. As we've seen, gastric emptying of sports drinks consumed during exercise is best promoted by maintaining a volume of liquid in the stomach, so it is advisable to drink every 10 or 15 minutes. The volume of each drink should be targeted to match your expected sweat loss for the conditions and the intensity of the training effort.

NUTRITIONAL STRATEGY DURING EXERCISE: KEY POINTS

- Consume small, regular feedings of carbohydrate (up to 1 g (0.04 oz) of carbohydrate per kg of body mass per hour).
- Ensure moderate concentration/ appropriate fluid balance (to replace sweat loss).
- Drink around 100–150 ml (4–6 fl oz) of fluid containing a 5–10 per cent carbohydrate solution every 10–15 minutes.

Nutrition for training camps and extreme long-distance rides

This section gives advice on those wanting to ride day after day with no rest days in between.

It's a situation you will find yourself in during a training camp, stage race or an extreme long-distance ride like the Race Across America. The advice here will also apply to anyone attempting to do the Land's End to John O'Groats ride in the UK, or a charity ride over many days.

Sportive riders preparing for a mid-summer event like the Étape or Gran Fondo Campagnolo will often go on a training camp in early spring. Some of the most popular are run by UK-based cycling holiday firm Graham Baxter Sporting Tours, which runs camps in Majorca. These camps are great if you come from northern Europe and have to struggle to do training rides in the early part of the year when the weather is cold and wet. A week or so in Majorca, southern France or Lanzarote offers warmer weather and access to long climbs that are comparable to those that riders face in the Étape or Gran Fondos. So they are a good way to supplement your training if you have the time and funds.

However, there is a word of warning. It is common for riders to go to these training camps and get carried away with the experience. On a training camp you will usually be riding with a lot of other keen club riders, all of whom are eager to make the most of the warm weather and mountain roads. This will usually mean training a lot harder on consecutive days than you would have done if you had stayed at home. That's a good thing because it helps motivation, but it also means that recovering after each session becomes even more important. A rider on a training camp doing rides of between four and five hours on consecutive days may need as much as 500–800 g of carbohydrate per day if they are to recover adequately. This will mean a massive increase in solid food intake, which for most people is simply not practical or palatable.

In such cases, the solution is to supplement the normal dietary intake with high carbohydrate energy drinks and snacks. In addition to the normal eating pattern, carbohydrate should be consumed in small amounts at regular intervals, both on and off the bike. The use and timing of recovery products is also vital for this sort of riding.

One of the major issues surrounding such heavy days of repeated riding is that athletes can suffer from a range of problems including: poor sleep; sore muscles and a feeling of restless or heavy legs; mood swings and hormonal imbalances; and a suppressed immune system. These are all classic symptoms of overtraining. This can often be seen when returning from the training camp. With the additional stresses of air travel, athletes come down with minor illnesses such as sore throats, coughs or colds.

An as yet unpublished study has suggested that a supplement, Science in Sport's Nocté, with its mix of protein as well as micronutrients to aid the recovery process and promote sleep, has a significant benefit. The key findings of the research indicate that taking Nocté before sleep tended to reduce muscle soreness. Equally important is the effect that Nocté appeared to have on helping to boost the body's immune

system. Further, athletes using Nocté were actually able to train more than their counterparts who were on a placebo.

Race day nutrition

Ideally, your race day nutrition strategy should actually begin a few days prior to your chosen event. Carbohydrate loading is something that has received a lot of publicity over the years, particularly in relation to marathon running. Years ago, marathon runners would drastically reduce their carbohydrate intake two weeks before a race while continuing to train as normal. After a week on this regime, the runner's stores of glycogen would be completely exhausted – as would the runner! A week before the race, the athlete would then load up on a high carbohydrate diet right up to race day.

The theory was that the carbohydrate starvation process would cause the body to crave carbohydrates. Thus, when a high carbohydrate diet was introduced after a week, it would result in a significant increase in the amount of carbohydrate that could be stored. This would mean that more glycogen would be available for use in the race, or so it was thought.

More recent research suggests that there is no significant gain to be had from carbohydrate loading in this way. It is much better to simply increase your carbohydrate intake in the week before a race, while reducing the training load. This has the same benefit as the old-fashioned carbohydrate loading method, but without the negative effects of the athlete feeling run-down and lethargic for a week, and struggling to maintain any meaningful training regime due to a lack of available energy.

So, in the week before a race, reduce the training load and gradually increase your carbohydrate intake. In the final two to three days pre-event, aim to get that up to 10 or 12 g of carbohydrate per kilogram of body weight per day. By doing this, the muscles super-compensate; that is, they become loaded with a much higher level of glycogen than normal.

There are, however, some drawbacks to be aware of. You are likely to feel very heavy-legged in the few days prior to the race. This is due to increased water absorption caused by the raised glycogen levels in the muscle. This is a perfectly normal sensation, but it is worth putting up with because it means that you go into the race with as much carbohydrate on board as possible.

Care must also be taken with regard to the source and timing of carbohydrate loading. If large amounts of fructose (fruit sugars) are consumed, or large amounts of carbohydrate ingested at any one time, the body may struggle to cope. If this then reaches the lower intestine, the bacteria will have a field day and the most likely result is diarrhoea! Not ideal as pre-race preparation.

During the race

Sportives can last up to 10 hours, or even more in the case of some of the Étape du Tour's

CARBOHYDRATE LOADING: KEY POINTS

- Reduce your training load over the final week.
- Gradually increase dietary carbohydrates.
- In the final two or three days, carbohydrate intake should reach 10–12 g per kg body mass.
- Carbohydrate loading may cause unwelcome side-effects.

longest stages. Getting enough energy and fluid on board is crucial if you are to perform at your best on race day. Remember: solid foods may take longer to digest than food in liquid or gel form.

It is perfectly possible to take on board enough energy for a ride of 10 hours or more simply by using energy drinks and gels. However, some individuals will find this difficult for two reasons. The first is that they may have a sensitive stomach that cannot cope with litre after litre of energy products.

The second reason is that we like eating solid food. Sipping energy drinks gets boring for many of us after a couple of hours and there is a psychological boost to be had from eating sports energy bars, sandwiches or cakes. It doesn't matter how stale the bread is in the sandwiches either; if you are hungry they can taste great.

TRAINING TIP: RACE STRATEGY

It is always very wise to determine, and then practise, your nutritional strategy prior to race day. Have a number of different strategies planned to accommodate the various weather conditions you may encounter (heat, cold, and humidity) and the distance of the event. On the morning of the big day (or the evening of the previous day if it is an early start), choose the most appropriate and try to stick to it.

Your strategy should include:
- **What to eat and drink**. This should take into account what you are able to carry with you, and what is available on feed stations. You should be comfortable in the knowledge that any foods or beverages you consume during the event will agree with you. *Never try something new on race day.* If necessary, find out what energy drink is provided, get a small supply and train with it to make sure you don't get any gastric disturbance. Similarly, just because the locals stop for a bowl of granny's home-made broth, doesn't mean you'll get on with it.
- **When to eat and drink**. Timing of fluid and food intake should be, as we have suggested, at regular intervals. But you also need to be flexible. Drinking every 10 minutes is a great way to stay hydrated, but may be rather difficult while descending a windy mountain road at 80 km/h (around 50 mph)! Plan your strategy to take account of difficult sections of the ride and the location of feed stations. And remember, don't get caught up in the atmosphere and miss your planned early intake. You may come to regret it towards the end of the ride.

Co-author of this book Richard Allen remembers having a ham baguette at a feed station towards the end of the 238 km (148-mile) 2004 Étape du Tour, which is the longest stage ever used for that event. The baguette was hard enough to knock a nail in with, but at the time it tasted like a gourmet meal. The point is that some solid food is preferable for most of us during such a long ride, but you should remember that solid food can take longer to digest than food in liquid or gel form. So it's better to have the solid food in the first few hours of the ride when the physical demands aren't so great and your body is exercising at a low enough intensity that it can supply the stomach with enough blood to digest what you have eaten.

Later in the race, when you need the energy to be delivered at a much higher rate, having solid food won't have the impact on your performance you desire, because you simply won't be able to digest it in time for carbohydrates to be broken down and reach the muscles. Therefore, it may be worth relying on gels and sports energy drinks that can give you a vital and rapid boost in your performance towards the end of a long ride, when you most need it.

The pro's experience

Many of you will have watched stage races like the Tour de France and seen riders being handed *musettes* (food bags) at feed stations during the race. These usually contain fruit, paninis or sandwiches, which the riders eat during the race. They will, of course, also be handed energy drinks and gels.

It is important to point out that the solid food they consume during a stage is really there to help them on the following day of the race, not during the stage they are riding in. In a race like the Tour de France, riders must consume around 8000 calories per day. This means they have to eat as much and as often as possible. Solid food has to be consumed because energy drinks and gels don't contain enough vitamins and minerals to maintain health for a three-week race. If the Tour riders were to have solid food only at night time, they simply wouldn't be getting all of the nutrients they need to recover for each day of racing.

Also, elite riders like those in the Tour de France can ride along at 40 km/h (25 mph) without going anywhere near their threshold heart rate, so their bodies can cope with digesting food on the move. It is often said that the Tour is as much a test of strong stomachs as it is of strong legs. You have to be able to cope with eating 8,000 calories a day or you won't make it to Paris. But the sportive rider doesn't generally have to worry about the next day because most events last only one day.

Some sportive events are similar to stage races and in these it is worth considering a different approach to race day feeding and including more solid food during a ride, just as a Tour de France rider would.

Travel issues

Many of the sportives that you will be undertaking won't be on your doorstep. It is very important to consider issues that may arise because of travelling. Clearly an 'overnight' to do a sportive 100 or so miles from home is not going to have the same impact as travelling to do the Étape, Cape Argus in South Africa, or the Lake Taupo Challenge in New Zealand. However, they will all present you with challenges to your nutrition, so it's best to plan ahead. Ideally, you want everything to be as normal as possible. Just because you are in France doesn't mean that your pre-race meal has to be frogs' legs!

The main challenges that you are likely to face are the disruption to your normal routine; the unavailability of 'tried and tested' or familiar foods; and the often inflexible pattern of meal times imposed by the opening hours of your hotel or local restaurants. Riders doing the Étape often note that it is difficult to find breakfast with such an early start and the vast number of riders in the surrounding area. So why not plan ahead and take some breakfast cereal with you. Additionally, having a supply of spreads, such as jam or honey, some sports bars, dried fruits, and powdered energy drinks or liquid meal supplements may mean that all you need to source at your destination is water. This can take the stress out of a situation in which you may arrive at a destination in the middle of the night, following a travel delay, having to race the following morning.

Putting it into practice

So now you know what you should be doing to prepare for, and to recover from training. But how do you put it into practice when work and personal commitments get in the way? For example, if you have to train at 6 am before going to work, it may not be practical to get up at 4 am and have a meal before going training.

In this situation, taking a carbohydrate energy drink immediately before you ride may be the better option. Then follow the usual guidelines for nutrition during training, and make sure you have a recovery drink after your training session. Having a good meal the previous evening is also a good idea in order to provide the energy you require first thing the next morning.

Similarly, if you have to train after work you may not be back at home until 8 pm or 9 pm, meaning that your post-exercise meal would be consumed at around 11 pm or later. In this case, it may be better to have your normal recovery drink immediately after training, and a light snack half an hour or so later. On days when training will take place later in the day, it is better to have a big breakfast, a moderate lunch and maybe a late afternoon snack to keep your energy levels up. The key with all nutritional strategies is to find what works best for your particular circumstances.

14
NUTRITIONAL TARGETS

Assessing your needs

You should now know what to eat and when to eat, but how much should you be eating? There are two key targets for cyclists. The first is to replenish the energy used for daily activity and training, while maintaining body weight. The second target for some riders is to lose body fat for either health or performance benefits. Essentially, with the exception of some minor tweaks, the strategy for both objectives is the same. The difference is solely the current body fat in relation to the desired body fat target.

Assessing body composition
It is advantageous to assess body composition as part of a physiological analysis of any athlete. For a sportive cyclist facing a mountainous ride, it is especially important to work out if they are

carrying excess body fat. Being a good climber is about having a high power-to-weight ratio and this will be hampered if you are carrying excess body fat.

Many sports science facilities will use special body fat callipers to measure skin fold thickness at various points around the body (Figure 14.1). These measurements relate to the amount of subcutaneous fat. A number of theoretical formulae are then applied to the values to work out total body fat percentage.

While many like to know a body fat percentage, the sum of the skin fold values is now being used more frequently because this will show small changes in body composition with dietary intervention and training. This is considered one of the more practical, cost-effective and accurate ways of assessing body fat and these methods are used by coaches and physiologists at the elite level in many sports worldwide. As an ideal, a well-trained athlete would be looking for the sum of seven sites to be between 40 and 60 mm, while an elite endurance athlete would probably be targeting around 25–40 mm.

Figure 14.1 Dr Garry Palmer assessing the body fat of an elite footballer.

If you are unable to undergo such a test, there are other ways of making an assessment of your body fat percentage, although they may not be as accurate as a proper physiological test. It is also worth pointing out that most of us will have at least some fat we can safely lose. Most of us can tell whether we do by jumping up and down in front of a mirror (semi-naked), or by pinching a bit of fat around our waistline.

If you can't arrange a skin fold analysis, a measure of bioimpedance is cheap and widely available. Many chemists and sports retailers now sell scales that 'measure' body fat. These systems work by sending a small electrical current through the body. The current will pass through muscle and fat at different speeds and, by measuring how long it takes to pass through the body, the scales work out the ratio of muscle to fat. Because they do not take into account your levels of hydration (particularly as different levels of fluid can be stored in and around the cells), they can be inaccurate. However, even if the body fat figure is out, it will always be out. So you will be able to see if your body fat percentage is dropping over weeks and months of training, so long as you measure it at the same time of day and under the same conditions (for example, first thing in the morning following a rest day, and after a visit to the bathroom).

Certainly bioimpedance scales are a better way of assessing body composition than the BMI (body mass index) system. This is often used as a way of working out if someone is overweight and it works by comparing an individual's weight and height. The result it produces is then compared to a table indicating whether someone is of normal weight, overweight or obese. The problem is that it takes no account of whether someone has a muscular physique;

it only uses someone's weight. So a heavily muscled, very lean elite athlete can have a body mass index that would class them as being clinically obese.

Body fat targets

Once you have an idea of your current body fat, it is worth looking at how this relates to other athletes. This is a relatively simple exercise for male athletes, and classifications of body fat percentage can easily be found. An example of one classification used is highlighted in Table 14.1 below. In this example, the values for fat mass and lean body mass are also given for an 80 kg (176 lb) male.

Table 14.1 Classification of body fat percentages for male athletes

Body fat percentage	Classification	Approximate fat mass of an 80 kg (176 lb) individual	Approximate lean mass of an 80 kg (176 lb) individual
4–6%	Elite endurance athlete	4	76
8–10%	Ideal 'competitive' athlete	7	73
12–15%	Ideal normal population	11	69
15–18%	Average normal population	13	67
18–24%	Overweight	17	63
24–30%	Medically at risk	22	58
30% +	Morbidly obese	24	56

As the table shows, an individual with the body fat percentage of an elite endurance athlete is likely to be carrying almost 20 kg (44 lb) less fat than someone who is 'morbidly obese'. That is the weight of more than three bikes! Sadly, in the current climate an increasing number of males have over 30 per cent body fat. This includes some who exercise on a regular basis and successfully complete sportives! Similarly, the same comparison suggests that if those athletes were the same weight, the elite individual would have 20 kg (44 lb) more lean body mass. This would mostly be muscle mass, and this is also likely to be the reason these athletes can produce an exceptional amount of power!

Females, because of their genetic composition, have naturally higher body fat levels than their male counterparts. The provision of specific classifications is also somewhat controversial. The 'ideal' target body fat for an athletic female is often considered to be in the region of 15–18 per cent, and lean is considered to be around 18–22 per cent. However, many elite females have had body fat values recorded in single figures, though most are more likely to be around 10–12 per cent.

Unfortunately, unless dietary intakes are absolutely on target, menstrual disturbances are often observed when body fat drops below 18 per cent. The main focus when targeting an ideal body fat percentage for a female should be the maintenance of menstrual function, and therefore we suggest the minimum should be 18 per cent.

Knowing your current body fat, and having an idea of a sensible target for your performance level, will give you an idea of how much weight it will be possible to lose. Certainly, in longer or hilly sportives this will have a major impact on your performance ability. For example, an 80 kg (176 lb) male who is well within the range of the average population at 16.3 per cent body fat would be carrying 13 kg (28.6 lb) of fat. If he was able to reduce his body fat to 10 per cent, and still maintain the same lean body mass, he would reduce his fat mass, and total mass, by 5 kg (11 lb).

Diet diary

Many cyclists keep a training diary, but if you are going to improve your nutrition it is equally important to keep a record of what you are eating. You don't have to do it every day, but you do need to do it for at least one week to work out what your diet consists of right now.

In the longer term, it is useful to keep a record of your diet in the run-up to a major race. This will help you determine what works for you and what doesn't. However, in the initial phase of your training, you need to determine how much energy you require to cope with the programme you are undertaking. If you need to lose weight, it is a simple matter of making sure that the number of calories you take in is slightly less than the number you are burning up.

It really is as simple as that, but getting the numbers right is crucial. If you reduce your calorie intake by too much, you will impair your ability to train. You may cause your metabolism to slow down so much that it becomes impossible to lose weight at all. In the case of extremely low calorie diets, your body will switch into a kind of 'hibernation' mode in which more of the food you ingest is stored in fat than it normally would be. This is, of course, the exact opposite of what you are trying to achieve.

Calculating your needs

The first stage in calculating your specific energy requirements is to estimate your resting metabolic rate. Resting metabolic rate is the energy that the body requires during complete rest to sustain basic life function. Although it is possible to measure this under very controlled clinical conditions, predictive calculations for resting metabolic rate dependent on age and gender will give you a good starting point (Table 14.2).

For example, a 45-year-old male of 80 kg (176 lb) would multiply his current weight by 11.6, then add 879 to this total, giving a predicted resting metabolic rate of 1807 kcal per day.

The next stage is to use the predicted resting metabolic rate to calculate daily energy expenditure (Table 14.3). Daily energy expenditure is the energy needed to sustain the body through its daily activity, while remaining in a neutral energy balance (that is, without gaining or losing weight). Daily energy expenditure is calculated according to activity level throughout the day. Some measures incorporate physical training; however, we will add this on later.

For example, the 80 kg (176 lb) male with a resting metabolic rate of 1,807 kcal and a light lifestyle would require approximately 2,530 kcal per day.

Most individuals fall into the classification of a light lifestyle if they have predominantly inactive, office-based jobs that require little or no manual work. However, if you use this

Table 14.2 Prediction of resting metabolic rate

Age	Less than 18	18 to 30 years old	Over 30 years old
Male	(W*17.5) + 651	(W*15.3) + 679	(W*11.6) + 879
Female	(W*12.2) + 746	(W*14.7) + 496	(W*8.7) + 829

Where W is current body weight in kilograms

Table 14.3 Calculation of daily energy expenditure

Lifestyle	Light	Moderate	Heavy
	RMR*1.4	RMR*1.7	RMR*2.1

Where RMR is estimated resting metabolic rate

method of calculation, be aware that moving around the office, using the stairs, walking around the shops, or performing other daily tasks such as cooking or cleaning will not increase the energy required. Someone with a very physical job, undertaking a large amount of manual labour that means they have an increased heart rate and sweat rate for a predominant part of the working day, is more likely to be classified as having a heavy lifestyle.

Your sporting requirements

In order to identify your personal energy requirements, you also need to calculate the energy expenditure from your training. This is where things become increasingly tricky! As a good starting point, estimated energy expenditure for cycling can be calculated as following:
Energy (kcal) per minute = 0.1667*Weight + 0.1667

For the example of our 80 kg (176 lb) rider, this would equal approximately 13.5 kcal per minute of riding, or around 810 kcal per hour of training.

Again, when using this equation, the importance of a reduced weight during cycling becomes apparent. A reduction in body mass of 5 kg (11 lb) would mean a reduction in energy expenditure of 50 kcal per hour. Not a huge amount in a one-hour training session, but potentially make or break in a sportive lasting between eight and ten hours.

However, there is a problem with this formula. It is only an estimation. It is based on the assumption that a rider is averaging 26–30 km/h (around 16–19 mph) on a flat road and as a solo effort; or that they are riding within a group doing just over 32 km/h (around 20 mph). The calculation takes no account of: terrain (particularly the amount of time spent climbing, or the severity of a climb); environmental conditions (wind speed and direction in relation to the rider, or temperature); group dynamics; or maintenance of a constant pace. Therefore it can only be used as a starting point.

Similar formulae are available for different ride speeds, other sporting activities (running, gym work, and so) and even household chores (like washing up or cleaning the car). But remember: at best, these are only predictors. They could be wildly inaccurate because of many factors, including technique.

Ideally, each training session should be monitored for intensity using heart rate, and possibly GPS or power data, which can then be related back to the individual's measured maximum heart rate, resting heart rate, threshold levels, maximal oxygen consumption and riding efficiency in order to truly calculate the energy used for each training session.

Your daily requirements

In order to calculate your daily energy requirement from training, add up the total calories expended in a 'typical' training week. This should then be divided by seven to give your average daily need. For example, if our 80 kg (176 lb) athlete does six hours of training per week, this would work out as: 6 hr @ 810 per hour = 4,860 kcal per week or 695 kcal per day (on average).

Your daily training requirements should be added to your normal daily calorie needs to give the total of energy required. In the example above, this would be: 2,530 + 695 = 3,225 kcal.

Therefore, this individual would need to consume an estimated total of 3,225 kcal per day to provide all the energy required to maintain health, allow for growth and repair, and also to replenish energy stores following training.

Weight loss: a balancing act

Thus far, the energy calculations performed have been related to someone looking to maintain their natural body weight, and to be able to fully recover from training. So, what changes need to be made for the individual who is looking to lose fat mass?

Quite simply, nutrition is a balancing act. If an individual is looking to maintain their current weight, energy intake must equal energy expenditure. If they are looking to lose weight, energy intake should be lower than energy expenditure. The problem is: by how much?

Many riders wanting to lose weight believe that continuing to train while cutting out all of the carbohydrate from their diet will cause them to burn more fat. Remember, this is not the case. Carbohydrate has to be present in order to burn fat as a fuel.

Another consequence of low-carbohydrate diets is that the body will use protein from muscle as a fuel if there is not enough carbohydrate available. So if you're on a long training ride and run out of carbohydrate, the body will strip protein from muscle to provide energy, even though it is a much slower process.

This phenomenon is why riders on low-carbohydrate diets will often suffer severe muscle soreness and fatigue following hard training sessions. In extreme cases, endurance athletes have suffered heart problems as a result of being on low-carbohydrate diets for extended periods. When the body strips protein from muscle, it cannot differentiate between muscle types, possibly resulting in cardiac muscle being utilised. All of this emphasises the need for endurance athletes to maintain high levels of carbohydrate in their diet, to produce not just optimum performance in training and racing, but also to promote general health.

It cannot be stressed enough how important it is to get the energy balance right for both exercise recovery and weight loss. Therefore, in order to successfully achieve weight loss, the energy balance must be delicately tilted. Although the press may publish fantastic celebrity diets of just 1,500–2,000 kcal per day, this is not enough to sustain daily training and promote successful fat loss. The key is to do things slowly. Unfortunately, the spare tyre round your waist didn't appear overnight, and it won't vanish overnight either!

So, it's back to the calculation of daily requirements. For the athlete looking to maintain weight, the targets set should replenish all the energy expended, and the body should remain in static balance. For the athlete looking to lose weight, a reduction in total calories of no more than 15 per cent should be undertaken. For our example athlete on 3,225 kcal per day, this equates to a reduction in energy of 484 kcal per day. In this way, a slow and steady reduction of fat mass should be able to occur. Ideally, each week total body weight should drop by approximately 0.4 kg (about 1 lb). By ensuring this is undertaken with the correct balance of

nutrients, you should preserve muscle mass, fully restore daily carbohydrate stores, maintain body water, and only lose fat mass. Although greater reductions in energy may be tempting to achieve more rapid results, these often leave athletes tired, poorly recovered and, once they're back on a 'normal' eating strategy, back to the same or even an increased body weight.

If you try reducing your daily calorific total by 15 per cent and it leaves you with too little energy, try adjusting your diet until the calorific deficit is just 5 or 10 per cent using the same calculation process. Stick to this total until you reach your target weight, then begin to consume the appropriate daily calorific total for your weight.

Energy balance

You now have a daily calorific total, but we now need to work out how many of those calories should come in the form of carbohydrate, how many from protein and how many from fat. A review of the earlier chapters will remind you that, ideally, you should be aiming at around 60–75 per cent of the calorific total as carbohydrate. You should then aim to consume between 12 and 15 per cent of your daily energy requirement as protein. The remainder of your calorific total will be in the form of fat. An example of this can be seen in Table 14.4.

In order to undertake these calculations, first work out how much of your total energy requirements your targeted carbohydrate intake will amount to. For this example, 65 per cent of 3,225 kcal is 2,096 kcal. Next, to convert the

Table 14.4 An example of dietary balance for training

	g per kg per day	g	% of total energy	kcal
Target carbohydrate	6.55	524	65	2096
Target protein	1.4	112	13.9	448
Target fat		76	21.1	681
			Total energy:	3225

calorific value to grams of carbohydrate, divide by four (this same calculation works for protein too!): for example, 2,096/4 = 524 g (18.4 oz) of carbohydrate. The same calculation can then be undertaken for protein required. To calculate the total of fat allowance, the energy value needs to be divided by nine, in this example resulting in a daily allowance of 76 g (2.7 oz) of fat per day.

At this point, it is back to the diet diary to see what you are currently consuming, and where improvements can be made.

Best practice

Unfortunately, just eating the correct balance of nutrients isn't enough to bring the results you are looking for. For example, your nutritional balance could be spot on, but if you consume all your daily calories in one sitting, the body would not be able to cope. Carbohydrate storage would be incomplete, the body would not be able to process the large amount of protein, and excess energy would be converted and stored as fat. Consequently, you would never be able to achieve the body composition you were aiming for. Best practice must therefore be followed wherever possible.

Ideally, you should look to eat smaller amounts on a regular basis. Some nutritional practitioners even suggest having five or six smaller meals a day. This allows for a steady flow of energy to the body, avoiding any highs and lows, and means the energy can be processed and stored at a sensible rate. Similarly, current thinking is also that the body cannot optimally tolerate any more than 25–30 g of protein per serving.

Therefore, look to spread your protein needs throughout the day if at all possible.

Consider eating what you want when you want, and also eat slowly and enjoy your food. This may sound dangerous, but if you eat when you are hungry, you will provide the body with the energy it needs, when it needs it. Also if you eat slowly, taking time to savour and enjoy what you are eating, the body has time to recognise that you are providing it with energy, and it will give you plenty of notice when you have replenished sufficient needs. In the same way, avoid getting overly hungry. In this situation, many people then rush their food and overeat. If the stomach gets used to being 'overly full', your body will not so easily recognise the signs that you have actually consumed sufficient amounts of energy.

Finally, avoid consuming a large amount of energy late into the evening (this includes the energy from your favourite alcoholic tipple!).

Your metabolic rate slows as the day goes on. A large meal late in the day may not be fully absorbed due to the slowing in metabolic rate. Excess calories will then be converted and stored as fat, again making it hard to recover or achieve fat mass targets. If you do find you have to train late in the day, a post-exercise snack should still be consumed, but the best practice would be to 'front-load' the day with your nutritional needs.

As with the rest of the advice in this book, these are just guidelines to get you started. Everyone is different, and therefore no two strategies will give exactly the same results in different individuals. You will need to modify the advice to see what is most beneficial for your training, lifestyle and body. Continually review how things are progressing and you will undoubtedly find what works best for you, and thereby gain the greatest improvements.

4

THE BIG DAY

15

THE RIDE OF YOUR LIFE

'Pain is temporary, quitting lasts forever.'
Seven-times Tour de France champion Lance
Armstrong

*'In cycling there are more bad times than
good times, but the good times make up for
the bad times*.' Tour de France and Giro
d'Italia stage winner Martin Earley on the
psychology of cycling

This is it. After months of training, the big day
is here. But the final preparations for your race
begin long before you actually get to the start
line. Taking some time a few weeks before the
race to get your planning and preparation done
is well worth it. There's little point in training

for months for an event, only to see your race
ruined by something you have forgotten to
pack, or because your travel plans have not
been sorted out. In this chapter we will provide
you with a checklist, so that there is no room
for error.

What to take with you

This will of course depend on whether you are
competing near home or travelling abroad. If you
are racing abroad, take as many spares with you
as you can carry. If something is going to go
wrong with your bike or your kit, you need to
have spares ready to hand rather than go
rushing around an unfamiliar town looking for a
bike shop the day before the race.

SPARES AND TOOLS

If you have room, this is what we recommend you take:

Bike equipment
   Two spare tyres
   Four spare inner tubes (you can never
      have enough)
   Track pump
   Spare cleats
   Allen keys and toolkit (pliers, cable
      cutters, multi-tool device, pedal
      spanner)
   Spare gear and brake cables, cable
      ends
   Mini-pump
   Spare seat clamp bolt (these often fail
      when riders have to adjust their seat
      height to get the bike to fit in the bike
      bag)
   Spare chain and chain tool (or PowerLink,
      or similar connecting device)
   Chain oil/lubricant
   Cable ties (for attaching frame numbers)

Clothing
Racing jerseys and shorts (take enough
   to cover any training rides you may do)
Socks
Shoes (check cleats are not too worn,
   and replace two or three weeks before
   the event if necessary)
Rain jacket
Arm warmers
Leg warmers
Helmet
Under helmet skull cap
Racing mitts
Long-fingered gloves

Other kit and energy products
Bike bag/wheel bags
Water bottles
Bottle brush
Detergent for cleaning bottles
Washing powder for clothing
Energy gels
Energy drinks (in powder form)
Saddle pack
First aid kit (with antiseptic wash or
   cream, and bandages or other wound
   dressings for treating 'road rash')

Packing

A week before you go, especially if you are going abroad, it's best to have a 'dry run' to make sure you have everything you need and that you have room to carry it all. Start by getting together everything on our checklist.

Then get your bike bag and pack the bike in. Getting your bike into your bike bag, and especially a hard shell case, can be a tight squeeze. But once your machine is packed in, you will find there is a lot of room in there to store other stuff you need. A good tip is to put a hold-all of clothing in there, to save having to carry another bag.

If you are travelling by air, it's a good idea to weigh the whole thing before you go to make

MY BIKE BOX

Ever tried to do a jigsaw when you are tired, or in a rush? It doesn't happen! When you are tired, stressed or just in a hurry, the bits don't want to go in, but you know they will!

You may well feel the same after doing a 10-hour sportive. You know your transfer home leaves bright and early the next morning, but you are so tired from the ride that you don't have the mental capacity to work out how to get your bike, wheels, tools, shoes, clothes, souvenirs, the kilogram of cheese, presents for family and everything else you have back in the bike box.

So take a photo of how it all went in when you went to the race, it will give you a helping hand about how to pack for the way home. That way, you should get it all back in, stress free, and make sure your bike doesn't get damaged.

Figure 15.1 A typical bike box

sure you don't fall foul of excess baggage charges. The simplest way to do this is to stand on your bathroom scales on your own and then get on with the bike bag, and subtract the former figure from the latter.

Bike bags

There are many bike bags on the market, but essentially they come in just two types: so-called 'soft' bags and 'hard shell' types. For air travel, hard shell cases are recommended because they offer more protection against the often rough treatment of airport baggage handlers (especially if you have a carbon fibre frame). Bike cases can be expensive, but you may be able to hire them from some bike shops or travel firms.

Soft bike bags are fine if you are travelling by car or going on a coach trip abroad, as many riders do to the Étape du Tour with sporting tour companies. Many of these companies offer bike bags for hire too, but again, check well in advance.

The day before

If you are travelling abroad to race, you will probably arrive at least one day before the event, and preferably two or three days before. In races like the Étape du Tour, you will generally use this day to get to the start village, and pick up your race number and transponder (the electronic device worn around your ankle to allow for automatic tracking of your progress during the race.)

On the day before the race, you may want to do a bit of sight-seeing, but it's best to put this off until after the event. Resting before race day is vital. Remember the words of five times Tour de France winner Bernard Hinault – don't stand if you can sit down and don't sit down if you can lie down.

However, there are a few things you *must* make time for, and some things you need to be careful to avoid. First, you must *always* find time to unpack your bike and make sure it has survived the treatment of the airport baggage handlers.

Put the bike together to check the gears and brakes are set up correctly. Also check that the wheels are still true. Take a test ride – it only has to be a few hundred metres – and make sure the gears are working correctly and everything is tight and properly adjusted. You don't want to have to wait until you are climbing the first mountain pass of the day to find out that you can't change down from the 52chainring to the 39.

Events like the Étape will have a start village open the day before the race, where you will find service areas with professional mechanics on hand to sort out any problems. If this is not available, you will at least have a few hours to sort out any problems yourself or find a bike shop. Before you set off, and again especially if you are going abroad, it's a good idea to search the internet for bike shops near to where you will be staying. That way, if something does go wrong, you can quickly get a lift to the shop for any spares or servicing that you need.

Once your bike is tuned up and ready to ride, you may wish to cycle to the start village, especially if you have spent a long time driving the day before or have been sitting in cramped airplane seats. A short ride the day before a race is fine and it will help you get your legs turning over after a long journey. But this should be a very light ride of between 20 and 40 minutes at recovery ride intensity and without any hill. Keep the gears low and spin at a high cadence. If this ride is taking place on the day before the race then it may be better just to rest.

Remember the rules laid down in the nutrition section about the importance of getting as much carbohydrate on board in the days leading up to the race. The day before the race is about resting as much as possible and eating as much high-carbohydrate food as you feel comfortable with.

Leave yourself a note

Knowing the route you will ride in detail is an essential part of your preparation. You should have studied the route many months before, because knowing the challenge you will face is an essential prerequisite to structuring your training programme.

For a sportive like the Étape du Tour, having detailed information about the race route is also a valuable aid on the day of the race. Knowing

A WORD OF WARNING

Before the Étape and other events, you will find a lot of riders want to cycle to the start village and it is natural to want to tag along. But, as co-author Richard Allen found out in the 2003 Étape in the Pyrenees, such rides can turn out to be a mistake. In 2003 the ride to and from the start village ended up as a 105 km (65 miles) trek with temperatures of more than 90°F. On the way back, there was a group of 30 riders and, as so many of them had pent-up energy after months of training, the inevitable happened. Competitive instincts took over and before anyone realised, the group was hammering through the foothills of the Pyrenees at 50 km/h (30 mph). By the time everyone got back to the hotel, many felt they had done the Étape already!

Needless to say, Richard and others in the group paid for their efforts in the race. Learn from their mistakes and make sure you know exactly how far you are going to have to ride. Anything more than 20 km (12 miles) and you are better off going by car. And if you do cycle, don't be tempted into racing against others; save that for the big day. There are no medals for being first home on a training ride the day before the race.

the race distance, when you are going to hit a big climb and the length and gradient of the climb is a great advantage. If you take a look at the bikes of pro riders before a mountain stage of the Tour de France, you will see that many of them have a piece of paper stuck to their handlebar stem. On it is a little diagram of that day's race profile telling them where and how long the climbs are. It saves riders having to memorise the stage route, or having to rely on team managers to tell them the details on the road. Making a note for yourself and sticking it to your handlebar stem is a great idea because it means you can constantly check where you are and what challenges are around the corner.

But remember, to make this information useful your cycle computer has to be calibrated correctly. Otherwise you may find that the start of a climb doesn't appear quite when you expect it to! It's also worth remembering that most races that have distance markers on the route will be measured in kilometres. So if you have your computer set to miles, it's worth changing it to kilometres before race day or you will spend most of the ride trying to convert kilometres to miles rather than concentrating on what you are doing. Ideally, you should get used to clocking up kilometres instead of miles to give yourself a chance to get used to thinking in metric. Of course, you could get into the mindset of the continental pro and log all of your training in kilometres.

Race day nutrition strategies

Sportive rides like those in the UCI Golden Bike series are well organised and you will find several feeding stations along the route. As well as water and energy drinks, most big sportives will provide riders with fruit, sandwiches and cakes, so you will have plenty of ways to top up your carbohydrate stores during the ride. The only problem is that, unless you are in the first group of riders, you will find that the feed stations are chaotic and you will be held up waiting to get what you want. So it's still worth taking with you energy gels and powdered energy products ready to dilute with water (a good choice in hot conditions is Science in Sport GO powder, which you can get in small sachets).

In certain conditions, if the weather is not too hot and the distance between feed stations is short, it may be worth missing out one station to save time. Alternatively, you could get friends to hand you drinks and food at pre-determined points on the course; although in big events, if you are one of the elite riders in with a chance of victory, you may find you are penalised by the commissaries. Further down the field, it is unlikely that you will suffer any penalties as a result.

There is another option for those who have some good friends who are prepared to act as domestiques and sacrifice their own chances for your benefit. Get them to ride the race and drop back to get food and water while you carry on riding. They then catch up to supply you with what you need. One former racing driver reputably employs this tactic in the Étape du Tour to great effect!

Race tactics

After completing your training, you may be good enough to go to a big international event like the Étape du Tour and be in contention for victory. Although it is a sportive ride, it is also a race in its own right and a prestigious one to win. Several young pro riders have won the Étape and then gone on to ride the Tour de France proper.

For most of you though, the sportive ride experience will be about getting to the finish as quickly as possible. Therefore you may think that race tactics aren't as important to you as they would be to someone aiming to win. That may be so, but it is still worth considering your tactical approach to the ride. Maybe you have set yourself a target of achieving a particular finishing time or race position. Whatever your aim, it will be affected by those riders around you.

You can be in the best shape of your life and hoping for a gold medal performance in the Étape but, if you get held up by a bottleneck of riders walking up the first big climb, all your training will count for nothing. So tactics can play a part. Let's have a look at a few common scenarios that are worth thinking about.

Pacing

From the training you have done, the best approach to race day is to maintain as even a pace as possible. There's no point in sprinting away from the start line; this will cause you to go into oxygen debt and fatigue far earlier in the ride than necessary. Maintain an even pace on the flat sections and then, if you have the fitness, ride a little harder on the climbs where you can make up more time.

Training partners

Many of you will have a buddy who you have spent countless hours training alongside in the build-up to a big event. Finding someone to share those long rides with is great for motivation. Often training partners end up targeting the same event and may have a plan to ride the event together.

That's fine, if you both agree to help each other on the day regardless of the difference in ability. But it is worth being aware that no two riders will ever perform at the same level. There will always be one who is stronger than the other. Having a rider who struggles on climbs riding flat out on a mountain pass to keep up with his super-climbing partner is guaranteed to test even the strongest friendship!

If you want to ride the whole distance with someone, you have to agree the rules beforehand. You must accept that the stronger rider is going to have to slow down to allow the weaker rider to keep pace. If you want to go for a time, it's best just to set off at your own pace and meet up after the finish. Some of our clients have started sportive rides with a friend, lost contact with each other in the opening kilometres and not seen each other again until the finish – and then realised that they crossed the line only a minute or so apart! It's a good idea to have a plan about where to meet after the ride and have a back up if Plan A fails. Taking your mobile phones with you is the best bet, but make sure you have network coverage if you are abroad.

Drafting

Drafting is when one cyclist rides behind another and takes advantage of their slipstream. When you are riding at more than 27 km/h (17 mph) on the flat, most of the energy you expend on the bike will go towards overcoming wind resistance or drag. Riding behind another cyclist, or at the back of a group, means you can ride at a lower heart rate and thus save a lot of energy. This is significant on a long ride.

Data from scientific studies has clearly demonstrated the advantageous effects of 'drafting'. For example, it has been shown that at speeds of 40 km/h (25 mph), a cyclist riding at the back of an eight-man pack can reduce his/her oxygen cost by up to 39 per cent. This energy saving allows riders working as a group to ride up to 5 km/h (3 mph) faster than a single rider. So it makes sense to ride behind others as much as possible.

Cycling etiquette dictates that, if you are in a small group, you should share the pace at the front when you have the energy to do so. If you go to the Étape du Tour and tag on to the back of a group of six riders who are sharing the pace at the front, you will be expected to share the pace too. It's called 'doing your turn'. If you sit at the back of a group for mile after mile, you may find that you soon learn a few new swear words in several different languages! You will have earned yourself an unwelcome reputation as a 'wheel sucker'.

Not doing your turn may also cause the other riders to try to drop you from the group, which may leave you riding many miles alone if there are no other groups coming up behind. So it's best to share the pace; by doing a little work at the front now and again, you will usually find that you go much faster than if you were riding alone. However, there may come a point on a climb where you find that you are losing contact with a group that has been riding fast on the flat.

On the other hand, don't fall into the trap of enjoying the feeling of towing the peloton along for mile after mile. You may get a buzz from receiving the biggest cheer in every village you pass through, but there are no prizes for being a 'bunch engine'. All that will happen is that you will run out of steam a lot sooner than other riders in your group. Even if you have done a lot of work, they may not wait if you get dropped. Trying to stay in touch with the group may mean you having to make a near maximal effort.

As we have discussed earlier, you should try to maintain an even pace because this makes the most efficient use of the energy you have available. But riding with a group is more efficient than riding on your own. So what should you do?

This decision has to be made on the road, and every situation will be different. But here are the factors you should consider. How far have you got to go to the finish, and are there any more climbs? If you make an all-out effort to stay with the group, only to be dropped again a few miles down the road on the next climb, then the effort may not be worth it. You may be left riding alone, exhausted by sprinting to stay with the group. If you approach the top of a climb and are losing touch with a group, it may be worth looking back down the road to see if there are any other groups coming up. If so, it may be better to let them catch you and ride with them instead.

If you have ever watched the Tour de France, you will have seen that cycling is a tremendously tactical sport, with dozens of factors to be considered in different situations. For the sportive rider, an event like the Étape du Tour or Gran Fondo Campagnolo poses the same tactical dilemmas. All we can do here is highlight a few of the factors to consider. Making the right decisions out on the road will largely be a case of learning from experience. You will make mistakes; the key is to learn from them.

It's all in the mind

Whether you are a Tour de France champion or a novice sportive rider, you will experience pain when cycling hard. In the Étape du Tour this will happen most in the mountains. Riding for hundreds of kilometres up and down mountain passes is a test of physical fitness, but it is also a test of mental strength. At the elite level, riders are well-matched physically. What determines who wins on a given day will be

who is the best tactically, but also who can push themselves the hardest when the going gets tough.

If you are going to produce the best performance you are capable of, you need to have a plan for dealing with those moments when the pain and suffering you experience make you feel like giving up. Some riders are naturally more determined than others, but we can all learn some techniques that will help us get through those tough times.

Association and disassociation

These are two ways of dealing with the pain of cycling when you are at your physical limits.

If you are suffering on a long climb and decide to get through it by concentrating more on your pedalling technique or by concentrating on your breathing, that's associating with the pain. You are focusing on factors that affect your performance and that can have an effect on your speed up the climb.

Disassociation is finding something to concentrate on that is external to the feelings you are experiencing. For example, you may wish to count the white lines on the road as they pass under your wheels. You might focus on your cycle computer, aiming to keep going for one more kilometre and then setting yourself another goal as the kilometre ticks over on the computer display. Neither method is better than the other; it's a question of which one the individual finds works best for them.

Thinking ahead

There are also techniques that you can learn before you get to race day. One that can help in training and racing involves spending a little time practising a positive thinking routine. You need to do this when you have some time to relax and can lie down to be alone with your thoughts. Music may help. Think of a ride where you felt really strong, fit and full of energy. Remember how it felt when you turned the pedals, the feeling you had in your legs and how easy it was to accelerate up climbs and overtake other riders.

You want to tap into this feeling of being strong and confident when you experience moments of tiredness and weakness. To do this, you need a trigger. For example, the trigger could be the music you play when focusing on positive thinking. In a race, recalling the music or even humming it can help you concentrate on being positive and pushing through the pain.

Alternatively, you could get a brightly coloured square of paper and focus on that colour during your positive thinking session. When you have a race coming up, stick a similar square of paper on your handlebar stem. When the going gets tough, you can glance at the paper to tap into the feeling of strength and confidence when you need it most. It may sound unconventional, but it can work.

It's all over: how to recover

Never again! That's the first thought of many riders as they cross the finish line in a mixture of agony and ecstasy. That thought may stay with you for a few days as your legs and body slowly start to recover from the effort you have put in. But there will still be elation: you did it.

In an ideal world, you should now be following many of the strategies outlined earlier in the book: consume a recovery drink; have a light spin to clear your legs; drink plenty of fluids to rehydrate; maybe have a stretch or a massage. But after a big sportive that ideal world may be a million miles away. Because of the large number of entrants, you often won't easily be able to get to your pre-prepared recovery drink. You may be looking for friends that you did the event with, or relatives who have come to support you. The best advice is to get whatever you can to eat and drink. Soak up the atmosphere, and share your experiences with those around you. Recovery may take a few days longer than ideal but, with the big day over, you need to give yourself a recovery week, or two!

Figure 15.2 Finishing the Étape

CYCLING PSYCHOLOGY
by pro rider Mark Cavendish

When you watch aerial shots on TV of a stage of the Tour de France, it may look like it's a steady ride through the countryside. If it comes down to a sprint, it's a chaotic free-for-all before someone throws their arms in the air to celebrate victory. But down among the wheels, it's a five- or six-hour game of push and shove with riders riding elbow to elbow, desperately trying to stay near the front to avoid being held up by crashes. And the final sprint involves riders and managers playing a game of chess on wheels, each trying to outmanoeuvre the other in thought and deed.

As a sprinter, Mark Cavendish has to think ahead and think fast if he is to be in the right position at the right time in those crucial final kilometres. What he says about the psychology of cycling demonstrates that we can all benefit from taking time to think about how we prepare mentally. So, what does it take to be a top road sprinter and how does Cavendish hone his mental skills?

'To win sprints, you need to be naturally quick; you need the fast leg speed to be there,' says Cav. 'But after that, most of it is about getting the tactics right and having the balls to go for it. To me, it's similar to chess. I used to play quite a lot and when I was at the Great Britain Olympic Academy I taught a lot of the lads to play. We played it in a certain style where you have to make your move within 10 seconds. If you take too long, you know that you will lose. It gets you thinking quickly and three moves ahead.'

For Cavendish, there is a parallel between the tactics of playing speed chess and a sprint for the line. It's not just about instinct. It's about planning ahead, rehearsing scenarios in your mind long before you reach the end game.

'In chess you have to think of the consequences of every move you make. It's exactly the same on a bike; you have to think about how what you do on one corner affects how you take the next corner.' It's all about working out where you want to be for the finale, making fast decisions when you get there and being ready for anything your opponents might do.

On a chess board, the cost of losing is a dent to your pride. On a bike at up to 50 mph (80 km/h) in a sprint, it could cost you your life. Whose wheel do you follow? Can you squeeze through that gap? When do you make your kick for the line? All of these questions must be answered in a split second. And the decisions made will have consequences that you must be ready to react to. Decisions like this, whether it's in a sprint or going into a corner on a fast descent, can make the difference between kissing the girl on the winner's podium and kissing the tarmac.

Cavendish believes that playing chess sharpens his mind and improves his speed of thought, helping him to react quicker when under pressure in a race. When he's not playing chess and has time to kill, you will often see him doing sudoku puzzles.

And what about that fear in the back of your mind that you might crash and end your career or even worse? 'You just don't think about it,' says Cav. 'There's a hell of a lot of riders who do think like that and that works in my favour. It's kill or be killed really.' And this is in the final few hundred metres. To get to this position, you have to ride anything from 160 to 260 km (100–160 miles) to even be in with a chance of winning the sprint.

Cavendish and his sprint rivals aim to save as much energy as possible by sitting in the slipstream of other riders to conserve the maximum amount of energy for the finale. He describes it as 'the sugar cube' – the amount of energy you have available at any one time. 'Throughout the race you are thinking about conserving energy. You want to have as big a sugar cube as you can at the end of the race.'

The mind is a powerful tool and if top pro riders like Cavendish spend time rehearsing mental techniques and thinking about their tactics before a race, you should too. Cavendish's focus is on being able to react more quickly in a sprint, but sportive riders also need to have quick reactions. In continental sportives, you may be descending at up to 95 km/h (60 mph). If something unexpected happens, like hitting a patch of gravel or a rider crashing up ahead, you must react quickly if you are to stay upright.

Being mentally ready for any eventuality, and knowing that you have developed your speed of thought and reaction time, can pay dividends on the road. It's worth thinking about.

In the first few hours after the event, continue to eat and drink as much as you comfortably can. Try to keep moving so that your body stays loose, and think about your journey home. You may not feel like it if you are leaving the next day, but it may be sensible to pack your bike and as much as your kit as you physically can. After that, go and enjoy yourself with your fellow competitors. Share stories, relive your experiences and revel in the camaraderie. You may still be thinking 'never again', but it will make the event even more memorable.

Once back home, one of the first things many people do is look on the Internet for their results. A scan of the results in terms of overall, gender, and age placing, and an analysis of your race day, will often give an idea of where lessons can be learned, time gained, or strategies improved. This is where the motivation often starts to reappear and people start planning for the next 'big one', whether it be a repeat of the same sportive, a move to more 'competitive' racing, or another challenge such as Land's End to John o' Groats or an attempt at something new like a triathlon!

Whatever your choice, go back to basics. Make notes of what worked for you, and where improvements could have been made in training, nutrition or on race day. Then start planning for your next big day!

Good luck.

16

TEN WAYS TO GUARANTEE THAT YOU *WON'T* FINISH YOUR SPORTIVE RIDE!

1. Don't pay any thought to your training. Just go and ride the bike when you can. It'll be all right on the day.
2. Eat as much as you like. You'll be burning so many calories in training that it won't matter what you eat.
3. Don't worry about checking your bike before you travel to the race. There'll be a bike shop near the start if you need anything, and even if it is 7 am on a Sunday morning it'll still be open.
4. Back in the 1960s, Tour de France riders used to train without drinking water because they believed that their bodies would adapt to being constantly dehydrated. It didn't do them any harm, so don't worry if it's 35°C (95°F) in the shade and you've only got a 500 ml (16 fl oz) water bottle to last a six-hour ride.
5. Get a copy of a training plan from your favourite pro rider. Just because they are among the best in the world and are full-time athletes doesn't mean that you can't cope with the same training load. If you do the same training as Lance Armstrong, you'll win the Tour seven times: right?
6. Get a heart rate monitor. You don't have to work out how to use it; just wearing it and writing down your results will make you go faster.
7. If you start to feel really tired in the build-up to your race, it's probably because you are not training hard enough. If after doing 20 hours a week of interval training you are fatigued, doing 25 hours the next week will get you back on form.

8. Don't check your travel arrangements if you are going abroad to race. If you've spent a year training for one event, it's really not worth bothering to check that you can get to the start line on time.

9. Even if you've never ridden in a group before, you'll be right at home among the 8500 riders on the start line in the Étape du Tour. There's no need to practise group riding in training; just watch a couple of Tour de France DVDs before you go.

10. Every year in the Étape du Tour around 1,500 to 2,000 riders fail to finish. They're just unlucky; it's not down to lack of preparation or training. It won't happen to you, will it?

USEFUL WEBSITES

www.cycletour.co.za – **Cape Argus Pick 'n' Pay Cycle Tour**

www.gruyere-cycling-tour.ch – **Gruyère Cycling Tour**

www.riderman.de – **Rothaus Riderman**

www.cyclechallenge.com – **Wattyl Lake Taupo Cycle Challenge**

www.rvv.be – **Tour of Flanders**

www.quebrantahuesos.com – **Quebrantahuesos**

www.amstelgoldrace.nl – **Amstel Gold Race**

www.felicegimondi.it – **Felice Gimondi Internazionale**

www.cyclosport-ariegeoise.com – **l'Ariégeoise**

www.markcavendish.com – **Mark Cavendish's website, containing information about one of the world's leading young pro riders**

www.scienceinsport.com – **Website of leading sports nutrition company**

www.polar.fi – **Website of leading heart rate monitor manufacturer**

www.sportingtours.co.uk – **Graham Baxter Sporting Tours, prominent cycling tour and travel company**

www.letour.fr – **The official Tour de France website**

www.letapedutour.com – **The official Étape du Tour website**

www.etape.org.uk – **Website with useful information about previous Étape du Tours**

www.sportstest.co.uk – **The website for Sportstest Ltd, Garry Palmer's sports physiology company**

www.cyclosport.org – **Information about sportive rides around the world**

www.letapedelegende.com – **The Étape de Légende sportive website**

www.kreuzotter.de – **Useful website for calculating climbing speeds**

www.veloriders.co.uk – **Cycling forum useful for finding training groups or swapping information about sportive events**

www.britishcycling.org.uk – **Includes information about UK sportives**

www.wielerplaza.nl – **Cyclosportive calendar featuring over 600 events worldwide**

www.pedalpower.org.za – **Organisers of over 50 rides in South Africa every year, including the Cape Argus Pick 'n' Pay Cycle Tour**

www.summerofcycling.com – **Road and mountain bike events in Australia and New Zealand**

www.cyclingnz.com – **The website of cycling New Zealand**

www.cycling.org.au – **Cycling Australia is the principal body for competitive road cycling in Australia**

www.audax.uk.net – **Audax UK, listing all UK-based audax events**

www.audax.org.au – **The website of the Australian National Audax Cycling association; includes event calendar**

www.rusa.org – **Randonneurs USA**

www.audax-club-parisien.com – **Website for the parent organization of the allure libre style of randonneuring**

www.audax-uaf.com – **The official organisation for the original audax style**

www.jomcrae.co.uk – **Expert stretching and flexibility advice**

INDEX

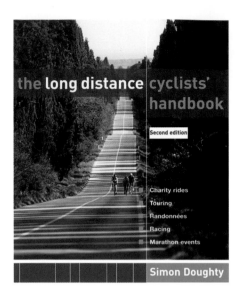

The Cyclist's Training Manual

The Cyclist's Training Manual is the definitive guide to fitness for cycling, suitable for everyone from complete beginners looking to build fitness for their first charity event through to experienced cyclists wanting to improve their competitive performance. This step-by-step handbook guides you through everything you need to know to train and compete at your best, including how to organise your training, training methods, nutrition, health and how to avoid the most common cycling injuries. It also provides specialised training programmes and techniques for all cycling disciplines, such as road racing, time trials, mountain biking, sprint rides and challenge rides, as well as specific advice for novices, juniors, women and veterans.

The Long Distance Cyclist's Handbook

Packed with straightforward information, *The Long Distance Cyclist's Handbook* details the preparation and equipment needed to take a novice from the challenge of a 50-mile charity ride to gearing up and comfortably covering 66 km in a weekend randonnée. It also tackles marathon events such as 12-hour time trials, and the ultimate test – the 3000-mile Race Across America.

Fully updated, this is essential reading for anyone contemplating a cycling holiday or any challenge that takes you outside your usual comfort zone. It brings you the most up-to-date information on training, technique, nutrition, health and travel, and combines the latest in sports science research with years of experience cycling beyond the horizon.

Triathlon

Triathlon is one of the fastest growing participation sports in the UK, attracting sportspeople from a wide range of backgrounds and fitness levels.

Triathlon begins with an overview of how to start out and what to expect, with clear and concise introductory sections to the three disciplines – swimming, cycling and running – including equipment, techniques, training and preparation. From this point, Mark Barfield's unique, easy-to-use and highly effective programme is designed to take even the beginner to triathlon success in just 20 weeks.

Packed with stunning colour images from an expert event photographer, with fascinating personal accounts of triathletes to spur you on and everything else you need to know about taking part in an event and the journey beyond, *Triathlon* is an invaluable resource for competitors everywhere.

Marathon Running

Written by Britain's most successful marathon runner of the 1990s, this invaluable guide will help you get the most from your distance training. From the complete beginner enchanted by the challenge of the London Marathon, to the experienced runner wishing to improve on racing strategy, its authoritative pages reveal a wealth of information on:

- structuring an effective build-up and taper
- training harder without doing too much
- improving your endurance and pace judgement
- producing your best on race-day.

The Complete Guide to Endurance Training

Endurance athletes, such as long-distance runners, cyclists, rowers and triathletes, have to train a lot – it comes with the territory. However, training by guesswork won't give you the best results for your efforts; training too often, too fast or haphazardly can lead to tiredness, injury and disappointment.

The Complete Guide to Endurance Training will teach you how to make the right training decisions, train smarter and achieve better results. Fully updated to take into account all the latest research, it includes 58 specific programmes to get you started, and tells you everything you need to know to customise them to your own needs.

The Complete Guide to Sports Nutrition

The Complete Guide to Sports Nutrition is the definitive practical handbook for anyone wanting a performance advantage. This fully updated and revised edition incorporates the latest cutting edge research. Written by one of the country's most respected sports nutritionists, it provides the latest research and information to help you succeed.

The 5th edition includes in-depth information and guidance on the following topics:
- maximising endurance, strength and performance
- how to calculate your optimal calorie, carbohydrate and protein requirements
- advice on improving body composition
- specific advice for women, children and vegetarians
- eating plans to cut body fat, gain muscle and prepare for competition.